The Chocolate Diaries

KAREN SCALF LINAMEN

The Chocolate Diaries

Secrets for a Sweeter Journey on the Rocky Road of Life

WaterBrook
PRESS

THE CHOCOLATE DIARIES
PUBLISHED BY WATERBROOK PRESS
12265 Oracle Boulevard, Suite 200
Colorado Springs, Colorado 80921

This book is not intended to replace the medical advice of a trained medical professional. Readers are advised to consult a physician or other qualified health-care professional regarding treatment of their medical problems. The author and publisher specifically disclaim liability, loss, or risk, personal or otherwise, which is incurred as a consequence, directly or indirectly, of the use or application of any of the contents of this book.

All Scripture quotations, unless otherwise indicated, are taken from the Holy Bible, New International Version®. NIV®. Copyright © 1973, 1978, 1984 by Biblica Inc.™ Used by permission of Zondervan. All rights reserved worldwide. www.zondervan.com. Scripture quotations marked (MSG) are taken from The Message by Eugene H. Peterson. Copyright © 1993, 1994, 1995, 1996, 2000, 2001, 2002. Used by permission of NavPress Publishing Group. All rights reserved. Scripture quotations marked (NLT) are taken from the Holy Bible, New Living Translation, copyright © 1996. Used by permission of Tyndale House Publishers Inc., Wheaton, Illinois 60189. All rights reserved.

Details in some anecdotes and stories have been changed to protect the identities of the persons involved.

ISBN 978-1-4000-7402-0
ISBN 978-0-307-72959-0 (electronic)

Cover design by Kelly L. Howard; photography by George Karl Groff

Published in the United States by WaterBrook Multnomah, an imprint of the Crown Publishing Group, a division of Random House Inc., New York.

Library of Congress Cataloging-in-Publication Data
Linamen, Karen Scalf, 1960–
    The chocolate diaries : secrets for a sweeter journey on the rocky road of life / Karen Scalf
Linamen. — 1st ed.
        p. cm.
    Includes bibliographical references.
    ISBN 978-1-4000-7402-0 — ISBN 978-0-307-72959-0 (ebk.)
  1. Self-help techniques. 2. Life skills. I. Title.
    BF632.L557 2011
    158—dc22
                            2010053730

Printed in the United States of America
2011—First Edition

10 9 8 7 6 5 4 3 2 1

SPECIAL SALES
Most WaterBrook Multnomah books are available at special quantity discounts when purchased in bulk by corporations, organizations, and special-interest groups. Custom imprinting or excerpting can also be done to fit special needs. For information, please e-mail SpecialMarkets@WaterBrookMultnomah.com or call 1-800-603-7051.

Contents

Nobody Knows the Truffles I've Seen

Bumpy roads may be inevitable, but misery is optional.

Two nights ago I discovered my fifteen-year-old in the kitchen at 3 a.m., whipping up pasta and shrimp in a garlic-and-lemon cream sauce. Blinking, I asked, "What are you doing?"

Kacie shrugged. "I couldn't sleep. I kept dreaming of recipes."

No surprise there. Kacie's gotten the whole family hooked on the Food Network. In fact, the kid has fallen in love not only with cooking but with Italian cuisine in general and with one teenaged Italian-bakery delivery boy in particular.

It all began when we started watching *Cake Boss,* a reality show recorded at a century-old bakery founded and run by a boisterous Italian family in New Jersey. One of the many relatives who works at Carlo's Bakery is seventeen-year-old Robert Faugno, nephew of Buddy Valastro, the master baker. Kacie is so taken with *Cake Boss,* the summer after she turns eighteen, she wants us to take a family trip to New

Jersey so she can visit the bakery and meet Robert (a.k.a. her future husband). Kacie's plan is to marry Robert and complete a brief pastry internship at the family bakery before the happy couple opens a Tuscan restaurant and starts giving birth to their own brood of boisterous future employees and reality TV stars.

Granted, Robert has yet to be informed of his pending engagement. But that's nothing more than a small glitch in the grand scheme of things. We tried to jump-start the relationship by looking for him on Facebook, but we couldn't find him. So if you happen to know Robert Faugno, would you please have him call Kacie?

I love that Kacie started watching the Food Network, fell in love with *Cake Boss,* and now sees her future life unfolding. I mean, what's not to like? You've got a big gregarious family. You've got festive events like weddings and bar mitzvahs. You've got chocolate.

Unfortunately, when I watch the Food Network, the programs that seem to best represent my life are part of a series called *Chopped.* In every episode up-and-coming chefs compete for ten thousand dollars by whipping up extravagant dishes in thirty minutes or less. The timer starts as each chef is given a basket containing three or four ingredients that *must* be included in the dish.

I'm not talking about flour, sugar, and eggs. These chefs have to create dishes using zany combinations such as oranges, grapefruit, and *bacon*! Or apples, shrimp, and peanut butter. My favorite episode is the one where the chefs are asked to create an appetizer with chocolate and sardines.

A tasty chocolate-and-fish appetizer. You should see the looks on their faces.

And then the timer starts.

Now *that's* real life. After all, you and I are given a limited amount of time on earth. (Sure, it's longer than thirty minutes, although we're never sure how much longer. Thirty years? Sixty? Ninety?) Then we're given a variety of zany ingredients with which to make something of our lives. Inevitably, some of the ingredients are things we don't want and may not even know how to handle.

Just yesterday a woman was telling me about her pending divorce. Through tears she said, "It's not what I thought I'd have to deal with in my life." I've had that same feeling. My guess is that you have too.

As we stare into the kitchens of our lives, we see all sorts of ingredients we didn't ask for. There are ingredients that don't play well with others and some that are downright unpleasant. We see signs of our

Sweet Secrets

Q: What's your secret to a sweeter journey on the rocky road of life?

A: I try to find others who need encouragement. So often my crisis becomes less of a crisis when I take my eyes off myself and look at the needs of those around me. You get to wallow in your crisis and have a pity party for yourself during the tough times, sure. But after that, you have to reach out to those who are in their own crises. That's when you realize that giving is the greater medicine.

—CINDI CHASE JOSEPH, CALIFORNIA

hard labor and great effort—scattered flour and dirty pans and potato peelings on the floor—but not always the results we long for. When this happens it's easy to become discouraged. We can even become convinced that we've been given such bitter ingredients that nothing can ever make our lives sweet again. (After all, it's hard to imagine even a skillful chef making something palatable out of a childhood hurt, a mistake from long ago, baggage from a difficult marriage, or lingering disappointment!)

But this philosophy suggests that the ingredients are more important than the life they produce. Don't believe it!

After all, Food Network chefs are routinely handed bizarre ingredients (such as sardines and chocolate) and manage to rise above their dismay to create the most amazing dishes despite haphazard combinations of flavors.

You might be thinking, *Well, of course they do. It's television! Even if it is a reality show, it's still entertainment.* And yet you and I know real people who exhibit the same talent, don't we? People who have been handed some *really* distasteful things yet have managed to fold them into the batter of their lives in such a way that the end results are not just appetizing, they're also amazing! These are people we love to be around, because their lives aren't characterized by bitterness despite the hardships they have experienced. Instead, they've extracted both the good and the bad from their pasts and blended it all to create lives that are rich and satisfying.

If you've never met anyone like this before, be patient, because in this book you will. Even better, these amazing folks are going to share their secrets for embracing a sweeter journey in spite of the rocky roads of life.

Some of the ingredients in our baskets are tasty. Others are bitter, and if they aren't handled well, they have the potential to overpower the entire recipe. And yet *if we know the secrets,* the bitter flavors can not only be tamed, sometimes they also end up being the very thing that transforms our efforts from ordinary to truly remarkable.

Not Exactly What I Had in Mind

I don't know a single person who hasn't traversed rocky roads (and I know only a few who aren't rattling over a few bumps even now). So why are you and I so surprised (or dismayed, or afraid, or even overwhelmed) when it happens to us?

We resist the bumpiness of life because it seems so unfair and it's always unwanted. But the truth is, rocky roads are inevitable. That's the bad news.

The good news is that even though hard times are unavoidable, the rockiest roads are veined with the greatest treasure, meant to be experienced fully and even mined for their riches.

A few months ago I tried to communicate this idea to one of my children. When Kacie complained that we were short on money, I assured her we were going to be fine, then went on to inform her that having too much month at the end of the checkbook was one of life's rocky challenges that I *wanted* her to experience!

Truth be told, I want each of my daughters to know what it feels like to

- have ten bucks in your account until payday and have to figure out how to manage until then.
- fight with someone you love, then experience the joy of discovering how to forgive each other, resolve things, and move forward.

- become frustrated with a messy house, then enjoy the satisfying feeling of bringing order back into your world.
- be stressed and figure out how to reclaim peace.
- experience the mountain peaks of love and the deep valleys of loss, and discover how to find beauty in *every* landscape and terrain of the soul.

We can't escape it. Life brings these challenges many times over, and I want my daughters to have the moxie to know how to handle them as they arise. I also want my daughters to be women of depth and wisdom, traits that are rarely picked up along the broad, smooth, easy highway of life.

Depth and wisdom are most often discovered as we stumble along dim and twisting back roads, trying to find our way back home. As much as we wish these treasures could be gleaned from comfort and success, the truth is that the bumpier roads offer the richer rewards.

Some days I understand all of this. That's when I say things to my kids like, "Rocky roads are chock-full of treasure. Grab a spoon and dig in!" On other days, however, I lose my bearings, and the *last* thing I want to do is celebrate the mettle-producing benefits of difficult terrain. On those days, I may be reeling because my own rocky roads have taken sharp, unexpected turns. I feel lost and overwhelmed, my journey suddenly turning dark and disenchanting. For that moment I'm no longer a member of the search and rescue team, but the one huddled under a tree, waiting for someone with a working compass to show up and encourage me toward home.

And yet this is what makes the adventure so very, very grand: we need one another! Whether we're high on living the sweet life or trudging fatigued on the ol' rocky road, we're not in this alone. Best yet, as we whisper to one another the encouraging secrets we've learned along the way, our journeys will be so much richer.

Java Therapy

A few weeks ago I had dinner with a couple of my girlfriends. We were in Debbie's dining room, enjoying a wonderful meal of bread and hummus and fruit. I'd just asked these women about their rocky roads. I wanted to know what they did to cope—no, wait, not just cope, but actually *thrive*—when life got hard.

Ronlyn knew about rocky roads. So did Debbie. So did I, for that matter. Among the three of us, we pretty much had all the bases covered, including single-parenting challenges, financial stress, career mishaps, depression, childhood trauma, health problems, and broken hearts.

"As you know," Ronlyn shared, "I went through a really tough time last year. But I think I began to cope—and really heal—in the Starbucks drive-through lane." (Now this is *my* kind of coping strategy! I waited eagerly for her to continue.)

"I'd been depressed," she reminded us, "really struggling with a lot of stuff going on in my life. One morning it dawned on me that if I didn't find a way to take my thoughts off my problems, I was going to drive myself crazy!"

An hour later, on her way to work, Ronlyn pulled into a Starbucks drive-through lane. Waiting in line, she had a crazy idea. When it was her turn to pay, she handed her debit card to the clerk taking orders at the window and, on a whim, announced: "I want to pay for the car behind me too."

And so Ronlyn's addiction began.

It started innocently enough with two or three random acts of Starbucks-drive-through kindness a week. Then she started looking for thrills in other places, like McDonald's and even Taco Bell. One afternoon she paid for the person in the car behind her while her kids were with her. And just like that, they were hooked too. Before long, her entire family couldn't get enough of the giddy rush of good deeds at drive-through lanes.

Not that there weren't sacrifices. Ronlyn, a single mom, never knew (until the deed was done, of course) if the driver behind her had ordered a cup of coffee or venti cappuccinos for the entire office. Sometimes the bill was a few bucks. Once it was nearly thirty.

This was not a cheap habit.

But maybe that was all right. It was cheaper than therapy. Plus, it gave Ronlyn a renewed sense of hope. Even though she was still living in her private quarters of stress and hurt, she had discovered a window to a happier world. And the more she created happiness for others, the more she found the courage to believe that happiness could exist in her future too.

Ronlyn couldn't stop smiling at the thought of how her newfound vice was impacting her innocent victims. As they drove away with their complimentary cup of joe or sausage biscuit, were they smiling? shaking their heads in grateful disbelief? Did they feel luckier or happier or even a little less invisible than when they'd rolled out of bed that morning? How were Ronlyn's random acts of drive-through kindness making a difference? She would never know.

Or would she? One morning on her way to work, Ronlyn pulled up to the Starbucks window and reached for her debit card. The clerk grinned and said, "There's no charge. The car in front just paid for your coffee."

I guess it's possible that nobody knows the troubles you've seen. But it's more likely that others have not only traveled the road you're on, they've also discovered a few secrets for making the journey a little sweeter. I believe your journey can be sweeter too.

You and I love our chocolate, don't we? Not the bitter stuff; we like our chocolate smooth and sweet. We want our lives smooth and sweet as well. Unfortunately, you may have learned, as I have, that it's a whole lot easier to control your choice of chocolate than your life.

And yet the next time life hands you a bitter ingredient, don't despair. After all, if sardines—with enough chocolate—have the makings of something truly amazing, think what hope there is for you and me!

Food for Thought

- ✎ Which reality TV show best portrays your life, and why?
- ✎ What are some unpleasant ingredients that you have had to fold into the batter of your life?
- ✎ Are you in danger of letting the bitterness of certain experiences overpower and define your life? If so, what are your other options?
- ✎ Has a friend ever shared something she learned from traveling her own rocky road that helped you get through a rough stretch? What did she share, and how did it help? Have you ever had that kind of impact on someone else?
- ✎ How did Ronlyn make her rocky journey a little sweeter? If you tried something similar, how might it help make your journey sweeter?

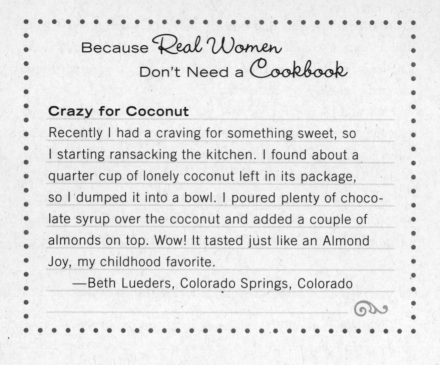

Because *Real Women*
Don't Need a *Cookbook*

Crazy for Coconut
Recently I had a craving for something sweet, so
I starting ransacking the kitchen. I found about a
quarter cup of lonely coconut left in its package,
so I dumped it into a bowl. I poured plenty of chocolate syrup over the coconut and added a couple of
almonds on top. Wow! It tasted just like an Almond
Joy, my childhood favorite.
　　—Beth Lueders, Colorado Springs, Colorado

Want More?
To find more chocolate recipes, or to post your
own, go to www.thechocolatediariesonline.com.

2

A Messy Kitchen: The Sign of Good Things to Come?

Sometimes healing starts when things are still in disarray—in a creative, messy place brimming with chaos and promise. Kind of like a kitchen.

Ask any woman about the time she felt the most broken, and she will tell you a story. It might be a story of love lost, financial hardship, debilitating depression, a father wound, a wayward husband, chronic pain, or broken dreams. Some women are still living their stories, wondering if their lives are broken beyond repair. Others have gone on to feel whole again.

All of which makes me wonder: how do women heal? And more important, why does tragedy make one person bitter and another better?

I love the story Ronlyn told in chapter 1 about her good deeds at drive-through windows! I love how—if we're simply open to the possibilities—almost anything can become an element of our healing, the ingredient that, folded into a bitter season, can change it into something new and rich and satisfying.

As Ronlyn shared her story, we were sitting at Debbie's finely set table, enjoying beautifully prepared dishes. And in that setting, we got to hear the story—and see some of the fruit—of Ronlyn's secret for a sweeter life.

But that's not where her story began. In fact, our stories of healing rarely begin at the banquet table where we share the fruit of our journeys. Instead, they usually start in disarray, in the tumultuous kitchen of our lives—in that creative, messy place brimming with chaos and promise.

It Started with a Shimmy

Having signed up for belly-dancing lessons, I arrived at the studio for the first class and found myself in an eclectic group of women. Middle-aged moms, tongue-pierced teens, menopausal hippies, and a couple of trophy wives mingled politely, if tentatively. One woman in particular caught my attention. She appeared to be in her late thirties, with long hair bleached white and lips painted black. The effect might have been intimidating if not for the fact that her lipstick was slightly crooked. She approached me and smiled. "I'm Phoenix," she said cheerfully. "I'm broken."

"Nice to meet you, Phoenix. Have you studied belly dancing before, or is this your first time?"

She waved her hand. "Oh, no. I've studied with all the really good teachers in Denver. I've never worked with this teacher before, but I hear she's very good."

"You said you were broken. How are things going? Are they getting any better?"

"I think so. Yes, things are better." She shrugged and smiled. "But I'm still broken."

Our instructor took command of the class at that moment, inviting us to sit cross-legged on the studio floor and take turns introducing ourselves to the rest of the group. Halfway through, it was my new friend's turn. She announced brightly, "Hi. I'm Phoenix. I'm broken."

Her real name is probably Barbara or Sue or Carol, but I like the idea that she prefers Phoenix. After all, since childhood I've been fascinated by the story of the mythical bird of the same name.

The phoenix, it is said, has the physique of an eagle and is adorned with beautiful red-gold and purple plumage. She has a lifespan of five hundred years, eventually becoming old and weary. Then, knowing she is nearing the end of her life, she readies herself for her final flight.

By now, of course, her feathers are tattered from centuries of wind. In fact, some of them are missing completely, having been plucked by treasure-seeking humans before she learned to isolate herself for protection. She even has a few scars from traps that tried to snare her.

Bone weary, she musters strength for her final journey. It's time to go home, to the nest on the face of the cliff where she was born. In flight, she approaches the cliff. Catching an updraft, she rises, then cuts into the wind, adjusting her direction before dropping altitude, her weary heart beating hard. Her destination—and her destiny—lies ahead. She tilts her wings to slow her descent. And then, in what can only be described as the ultimate crash and burn, she collapses into her nest and bursts into flames. Within minutes she is consumed by the fire. After a while the flames subside, embers flicker, and eventually nothing is left of our heroine except a pile of white ash.

The afternoon sun beats against the side of the cliff.

Aimless white clouds drift across the sky.

Then, in late afternoon, a breeze kicks up and blows across the nest. The ashes stir, then dance. In the movement, a shape emerges. Of cinder or flesh, it's hard to tell. It looks like a baby bird. She shakes off a powdery shroud and blinks at the sun. She feels the breeze and stretches virgin wings. She grows rapidly, reaching her full height within minutes. She is beautiful, with a young, strong body, bright eyes, and pristine feathers. In a sudden burst of strength and sinew, she beats at the air with her wings, scattering the last ashes from the nest. She rises, buoyed by muscle and current. Airborne now, her feathers glow magenta and plum in the afternoon sun. Reborn and renewed, she soars.

By the third week of class, I got to see Phoenix dance. She was beautiful. Tentative at times, but graceful. Made me think of ashes in the breeze.

It's an image I hang on to. Phoenix may still think of herself as broken, but I think she's gonna be okay. What's more, I feel honored that I had the privilege of meeting her—not at some point in the future as she looks back and tells the story of how she healed, but right here in the middle, or maybe even the beginning, of her transformation.

I've crashed and burned lots of times. Like Phoenix—and maybe even like you—I know what it feels like to have to reinvent my well-being and even my world from the ashes on up.

Looking for Signs of Life

One of my crash-and-burn experiences occurred about four years ago. I had recently moved from a suburb of Denver to a big house in the woods in Colorado Springs so I could live closer to my family. My new house was just a couple of miles from my parents', and from my sisters' too. They were so excited to have us nearby that Dad let me borrow his prized, one-ton truck and favorite trailer, plus a couple of hired hands, to help move my things. The move went smoothly (except for losing the metal gate off the back of Dad's trailer—yikes!) and seemed to herald the beginning of good things for my two daughters and me.

While I loved everything about my new life, there were things I missed from our old life in Denver. In fact, I was surprised how much I grieved losing those few things. The first was silly, when I think about it. But I really missed waking up and seeing the sunrise from my bedroom window. The second thing wasn't silly at all: I had left someone behind whom I loved. Even though he was making plans to follow me to Colorado Springs, I grieved his absence.

Six months after my move, that relationship ended on a dime. I was caught completely off guard. I felt numb and, at the same time, fully aware of the pulse of enormous pain throbbing just beneath the surface, like careless dental work as the anesthesia is wearing off.

My vision seemed different too. Whereas once I'd looked ahead and seen a future, at that time all I could see was hurt. There was no happy, healing ending in sight. If healing existed in my future (and it did, of course), I was convinced that it was far away, hidden beyond miles of road and hillocks and even a hairpin turn or two. Talk about a rocky road!

Just like an imagined Food Network version of my life, I had been handed a mess of bitter ingredients. I was stuck in a messy kitchen, surrounded by unfamiliar (and unwanted!) ingredients, with no clue how to transform the chaos into anything that might be the least bit satisfying.

The day the relationship ended, I went for a long walk: five, maybe six miles. I did the same thing the next day, and the day after that. Pushing my body past comfort and into pain provided a small distraction from the other pain, the one Epsom salts couldn't cure.

On the third morning I woke up early and groaned as my eyes adjusted to the pink morning light. Wait, pink light? Looking out my window I saw vivid strokes of sunrise across the horizon. I blinked. For the six months I'd lived here, the sun had always risen off stage, slightly past the edge of my bedroom-window view. Now, apparently thanks to the seasonal tilt of the earth, it was rising in plain sight, painting the

❧ Sweet Secrets ☙

Q: What's your secret to a sweeter journey on the rocky road of life?

A: I've certainly lived this in the past months. I have developed a routine of self-care that includes
- keeping up with my health and well-being through exercise, healthy diet, and plenty of rest.
- staying in the moment (not vainly imagining the worst for the future) by touching something within my reach in the here and now.
- confiding in a few very close friends for prayer and emotional support (and the occasional coffee, tea, lunch, or chocolate ☺).
- most important, staying in a really close relationship with God (prayer, study, and reading inspirational stuff).

—SHAREN WATSON

sky behind the pines with the glowing hues of dawn. The sunrise I had missed so much had come home, a bright and timely gift in the midst of my darkness.

That afternoon I struck out on another walk. On a whim I headed to my parents' house two miles away. They live on a quiet dirt road with little traffic. For most of the way, I walked with my eyes closed, looking for something I suspected couldn't be found anywhere except inside of me. And to be honest, I doubted that I'd find it even there.

Knowing I was approaching a slight bend in the road, I opened my eyes. I immediately caught the glint of sunlight on something in the tall weeds at the side of the road. I veered over to take a look.

There, in the ragweed and tall grass, was the lost gate from my dad's trailer! Apparently it had fallen off months earlier when we were driving down this gravel road to return the trailer to Dad's house. Seeing it lying there in the weeds, I rejoiced, then hurried to tell my dad the good news.

Something else unusual happened that week while I was still in the messy kitchen of my life. It was evening, and I was sitting in Starbucks with my friend Linda and my daughters. It was a half hour before closing, and we were drinking cappuccino and hot chocolate. That's when I noticed a man standing at the counter with his back to us.

I studied the familiar form. He turned and walked past us, toward the exit.

I began to laugh. "John?"

My old friend turned, spotted us, and grinned. The next thing I knew, I was in the middle of a big bear hug. No, it wasn't the boy I had left in Denver, but a good friend and former business partner. We'd had a blast working together for more than a year, until stressful events and an unfortunate tiff had driven us apart. And then I'd moved to Colorado Springs and he to California, and with nine hundred miles and the memory of frustrated words between us, reconciliation seemed unlikely.

About as unlikely as running into him now, in some random Starbucks.

"John, what in the world are you doing here?"

"I'm here on business and was driving through town on my way to Denver when I remembered there was this Starbucks not far off the freeway..."

We caught up briefly on each other's lives, hugged again, and promised to stay in touch. As soon as he was gone, one of my daughters looked at me with wide eyes. "I thought you guys were mad at each other!"

"We were."

"But you weren't mad just now. How come?"

I shrugged. "I think the crazy jolt of running into each other jarred us out of our ruts and reminded us that life was good when we were friends!"

"So you're not mad?"

"Nope."

"Not even a little?"

"Not even a little."

Back in the Kitchen

I pondered the events of that week for a very long time. I was still in a very messy kitchen. It would be months—more than a year, actually—before I'd find a way to put my heart and my life back in order.

But I had caught a glimpse of a potent truth. Sometimes you lose things and you grieve. You think the things you lost are gone forever, and in some cases they really are. But sometimes things lost can be found again. Like sunrises. And tailgates. And good friends. And definitely hope and joy, and maybe, one day, even love.

It was the kind of truth you can use to season a pot of bitter herbs, then let it simmer for a while. Eventually you end up with something palatable. Savory, even.

Maybe you've been handed your own bitter ingredients and you're not sure what to do next. I know it's scary, but don't despise the kitchen, that creative, messy space where good things begin.

Or perhaps you've crashed and burned and you feel like a pile of gray ash waiting for a life-giving breeze. Don't despair. Please, don't despair. Be patient. A wind will arise. It always does. And when it does, well, as our friend Phoenix is discovering, first you dance, then you fly.

Food for Thought

- ✑ If healing is a dance, where will you take your first steps? In a belly-dance studio? On a scenic trail? Toward an old friend in Starbucks? When you think of things that represent your first steps toward healing—recently or years ago—what comes to mind?

- ✑ Whether we're talking about making an exotic meal from scratch, redecorating a room, writing a book, crafting a sculpture, or even raising a kid, the creative process often feels overwhelming or ruined or even futile. In fact, it almost always feels that way right before a major breakthrough or flash of genius. But just because something *feels* overwhelming or hopeless doesn't mean it really is. Can you think of any times this has been true in your life?

∽ Have you ever crashed and burned? What was it like, and what is your life like today?

∽ If someone you loved admitted to you, "I feel like I'm broken and I'll never be whole again," what would you say?

Because *Real Women*
Don't Need a *Cookbook*

Homemade Peanut Butter Cup on a Spoon

When I need a chocolate 911, I start with a spoon. I use it to grab a spoonful of peanut butter, add mini chocolate chips on top, shove it in my mouth, and aah...instant heaven!

Mock Hot Fudge Sundae on a Spoon

Grab a jar of hot fudge and a spoon. Scoop up a spoonful of fudge, add some whipped cream from a can, top with a cherry, and you will absolutely drool!

—Michelle Morton, Raleigh, North Carolina

Michelle, I love the spoon theme! If I got in the habit of making sundaes in a spoon, instead of a mixing bowl, think how many calories I might save! —KSL

3

Chocolate and Other Affairs of the Heart

In case of heated argument, add chocolate. It makes everything sweeter and can help two people stick together.

One minute I was in the middle of a relaxed and happy conversation with my daughter, Kaitlyn, who was nineteen at the time. The next thing I knew, I was standing barefoot on the front deck shouting, "Fine! Be that way!" as Kaitlyn peeled out of my driveway in her Lumina.

I hate it when that happens.

I huffed back into the house. Needing something to fill the gaping, ripped-out place inside me, I popped a big bowl of popcorn, dumped in a bag of peanut M&M's, and poured myself a Fresca (diet, of course). Then I went to the phone and dialed Kaitlyn's cell phone.

"This is Kaitlyn," said a recording. "I can't come to the phone right now, so leave a message at the beep."

"Hi. It's me," I said. "Turn around and come home, okay? We won't talk about it. We won't talk about anything. We'll just eat popcorn and M&M's. I love you. Please come home."

Hanging up the phone, I glanced into the hallway and saw daylight. The front door was standing open. Apparently I'd forgotten to close it after my little hissy fit on the deck. I walked to the door, intending to push it closed, but swung it all the way open instead. Then I shuffled back to my popcorn and Fresca.

I called Kaitlyn several more times. Still no answer. Eventually I turned on my laptop and started writing her a letter:

> I won't let you go, Kaitlyn. You might think that you have
> the option of walking out of my life, but you don't. I won't let
> you go.

Someone was standing at my elbow. It was Gabriella, my six-year-old niece, who'd been playing upstairs with my daughter Kacie. Gabriella said, "Auntie Karen, the front door's open."

"I know."

"Should I close it?"

"No, sweetie, leave it open."

"Why do you want it open?"

It would have taken too long to explain, so I made something up. I said, "So I can see all the trees."

She went back to Kacie and her stuffed animals. I started typing again.

> Kaitlyn, sometimes loving takes practice. It means figuring
> out how (and when) to forgive and accept. It means learning
> how to give a little grace and a lot of love, even when the other

person isn't doing everything we want them to. It means
hanging on to each other, even when we're disappointed
or mad.

I stopped typing and stared at my phone, willing it to ring or vi-
brate or thumb its nose at me or something.
Nothing. I started typing again:

I wish I could be the perfect mother. I wish I didn't get
wounded, wound others, or make mistakes. But I do. That's
the bad news. The other bad news is that I'm the only mom
you've got. Can you find it in your heart, somewhere, to love
me even with all my shortcomings?

I heard buzzing and looked up. A wasp had flown in the open
door and was dancing dizzily in the fold of the draperies. Gabriella
must have heard him too, because a moment later she was at my elbow.
"Auntie Karen, a wasp got in the house."
"Yep, I see him."
"He came in the front door."
"He sure did."
"Can we close the door now, or do you still need to see all the
trees?"
I was watching the wasp. I envied him the simplicity of his di-
lemma. If he felt disoriented, he could thank his lucky stars he was
merely in the draperies and not in a relationship. Relationships can be
really dizzying. I mean, I'm a relationship person. I love people. Relationships are my drug of choice, my recreation, my passion. And sometimes they're too much for even me. I can't imagine how exasperating
they feel to a normal person.

This Crazy Little Thing Called Love

I remembered something that happened back when Kaitlyn was in third grade. She and several friends had been playing in the backyard when Kaitlyn, her face distorted with fury, stormed into the living room where I sat reading.

I put down my book and looked at my eight-year-old. I could practically see steam coming from her ears. I figured her friends had done something *really* terrible. Beyond name calling or quarreling. Something more along the lines of homicide or consorting with international terrorists.

I said, "What's the crime?"

Through clenched teeth Kaitlyn hissed, "They won't do what I want them to do!"

You can't blame an eight-year-old for not knowing how to handle all the emotions that emerge when people don't meet your expectations. You can't even blame a nineteen-year-old for struggling. In fact, even at my age, I'm still learning how to handle disappointment when people I love fall short of my expectations.

Oddly, my tiff with Kaitlyn on the day of the open front door was a reversal of the usual mom-daughter blowup. This time, she was upset at me for dating someone she didn't think was right for me. I was upset with her for not trusting my judgment. And then there was the bigger issue I suspected lay underneath everything, which wasn't the suitor-suitability question at all, but the sadness Kaitlyn felt over her parents' divorce.

The truth is, life has a way of going awry. Sometimes parents don't behave, no matter how well you raise them. Sometimes they do dumb things like get divorced. Sometimes they do even crazier things like date a thirty-two-year-old performance artist with multiple facial piercings. (I'm *kidding.* He was thirty-three.)

And even when parents aren't behaving in exasperating ways, you can count on children, friends, and even spouses to pick up the slack. Bottom line, it seems like—at any given moment in any given family, clique, or community—somebody's not doing what you want them to do. Which is fine if that person is your reclusive uncle Albert who lives on a fishing boat off the coast of Canada or the hairdresser you see just six times a year. But what if it's someone you're close to? someone you love? someone you really don't want to lose?

Vignette One: Healing from Past Hurts

After three years of marriage, Jarod and Ashley separated. He stayed in their apartment; she went to live with her parents. Reconciliation seemed unlikely.

A year later they began to talk seriously about getting back together. But now the road to reconciliation seemed rockier than ever. In addition to the need to resolve the original issues that had driven them apart, they now had another hurdle to get over: in Ashley's absence, Jarod had slept with another woman. Ashley was devastated; she'd expected Jarod to be patient while they worked things out. Jarod had figured that since they'd been planning to divorce, Ashley wouldn't care so much about what he did.

Talk about unmet expectations!

Six months later this couple renewed their vows before family and friends. Their secret for finding the bridge to a healed relationship? Ashley said that as much as they needed to work through painful issues, they had a greater need to be reminded of *why they should even bother*. Balancing the sweet and the bitter, they agreed to date each other several times a week. These dates were set aside for laughter and romance, for reliving good memories and making new ones. No serious conversations allowed!

Every Saturday, however, they walked to a park, found a quiet corner, and spread a blanket underneath some trees. Sitting on the blanket, they hashed out all the hurt. They vented, yelled, accused, and cried. They explained, apologized, and justified. Here, wrestling through the hard stuff was encouraged. Embraced, even. But only on that blanket.

Their dance between sweet and bitter went on for months. Eventually they forgave each other, folded up their little island of grievances, and never looked back.

Vignette Two: We All Rock the Boat

A very wise and beautiful woman named Meredith told me this story about her youth. When she was a teenager, she got into the kind of trouble that is common among girls: looking for love from the wrong kind of boys. What began as a short swim into enticing waters soon turned into a whirlpool of emotions and events she couldn't control.

When Meredith's parents discovered what was happening, they rushed to her rescue. For weeks there were long conversations in which emotions ran high. Anger. Remorse and forgiveness. Boundaries and grace. Grief and hope. Shame and relief. They all mingled and ran together, like a river of mascara and tears. Meredith knew the kind of life her parents wanted her to embrace. She wasn't sure, however, what kind of life *she* wanted to embrace.

One day she was at a store with her parents. They began visiting with a man their age, someone they knew. Meredith stared, enthralled. It was as if the man were lit from within, beaming from the inside out. What was it?

Meredith watched from a distance until her parents waved her closer. Introducing the man to Meredith, they mentioned that he was a pastor. Suddenly Meredith understood. She was drawn to this man because she was drawn to his Jesus.

Meredith had accepted Jesus into her heart as a child, but she hadn't given their relationship much thought for a long time. In a heartbeat, she knew what she wanted. She wanted Jesus. And she wanted other people to be able to look at her and see the light. She wanted them to see God inside her and to know that Someone cared about them.

ᘒ Sweet Secrets ᘒ

Q: What's your secret to a sweeter journey on the rocky road of life?

A: I do two things. I almost always pray first. I find such peace in turning my problems over to Someone who is much more capable than I am. In addition to prayer, I talk to the wisest people I know or to someone who might have insight into my particular problem so that I can work on problem solving as soon as possible.

—KELLY MCCURLEY, LARKSPUR, COLORADO

Meredith had turned a corner. But part of her was still mad at her parents—hurt by their reaction. Why had they been so hard on her? In the painful weeks after they had discovered Meredith's secret life of boys, there had been beacons of love and forgiveness in their eyes, to be sure. But Meredith could only seem to remember the flashes of hurt and disappointment.

One day her aunt told her, "Meredith, no one in a family is perfect. Not you; not even your parents. A family is a collection of imperfect people bound together by love, huddled in a boat, riding the stormy seas of life. You fell out of the boat, and currents were sweeping you toward the open sea. People who love you lunged over the side and grabbed you by the wrists and hair and pulled you back into the boat. And you're safe now—you won't perish at sea, thank God! But you've got a sprained wrist and a big headache. You've got wounds inflicted in love and rescue, but at least you're back in the boat!

"A family is a collection of imperfect people bound together by love, huddled in a boat, riding the stormy seas of life. And sometimes, to get to the other side, we have to be willing to understand and forgive."

Vignette Three: Eighteen Ways Love Is Just Like Chocolate

1. Everybody needs chocolate.
2. Chocolate can be bitter, although most of the time it's sweet.
3. The benefits of chocolate far outweigh the sacrifices.
4. Very few people will turn down the gift of chocolate.
5. Chocolate can get very, very messy.

6. Even when it's messy, chocolate is still very, very good.
7. Chocolate is habit forming.
8. Sometimes, bitter things, covered in chocolate, turn out better than you thought they would.
9. Chocolate can make things stick together.
10. Chocolate should be savored.
11. Chocolate makes the world go 'round.
12. Chocolate is a great remedy for the blues.
13. Chocolate may look a little different under heat and pressure, but it's still chocolate.
14. Chocolate can make you live longer.
15. There is no substitute for good chocolate.
16. Sometimes chocolate is good therapy.
17. Never take chocolate for granted.
18. You're never too old to be a connoisseur of fine chocolate.

Leave the Front Door Open

"Can we close the door now, or do you still need to see all the trees?"

Gabriella was still at my elbow, in the living room, waiting for my answer. I was still thinking about blankets in the park and a little boat being tossed by the ocean and the dizzying, imperfect journey of loving and being loved.

I was also thinking about trees. I remembered that I had told my niece I'd left the door open so I could see all the trees. Maybe my words held greater meaning than I'd intended. Maybe some conflicts are like a single scarred and stunted tree. Focus on that single twisted tree and you just might miss the beauty of the vibrant forest.

At that moment Gabriella and I heard the sound of a car pulling into the driveway. My niece and I stared at each other wide-eyed before she said, "Kaitlyn's home!"

We ran to the door and onto the deck; I stood at the railing, literally clapping my hands with glee. Kaitlyn sat in her car below me in the driveway, peering up at me through the windshield. Then she shook her head as if to say, *And they say teenagers are the crazy ones.*

After opening the car door, she stepped onto the driveway. I hollered over the railing, "I tried to call you."

"I know."

"I left the front door open for you."

"I see that."

"Do you want some chocolate?"

Within minutes Kaitlyn, Gabriella, and I were sitting in a pile on the couch, making short order of the bowl of popcorn and M&M's. After a while the bowl was empty and Gabriella went back upstairs. Kaitlyn and I looked at each other.

After a moment I said, "I'd love to tell you what the future holds, but honestly, I have no idea what our lives are going to look like five years from now or even five weeks."

"Me neither."

"Or what new people will be in my life or in yours."

Kaitlyn's bottom lip slid out past her upper. "But I like things the way they are. The way they were. Why do things always have to change?"

"I don't know." I held her hand. "But no matter what—no matter how things change or how we change or how disappointing it is when people we love do things we don't like—we have to promise each other one thing…"

We hooked pinkies.

"No matter what, we gotta always keep the front door open. And solve everything over chocolate."

"That's two things."

But the words kept spilling out like a river. "And we have to keep talking," I added, "and always love each other. And not give up. And be willing to listen and compromise. And keep talking and loving each other some more after that. And keep eating chocolate. And I guess after all that..."

The current of words began to slow. "After all that, if we do all that and it's not enough..." I tried to think of alternatives. I couldn't really come up with any.

Kaitlyn squeezed my hand. "If we do all that, Mom, it'll be enough."

Food for Thought

- ℰ Relationships can be messy. How do you know when a relationship is worth holding on to despite the effort required?

- ℰ How can you tell the difference between a healthy relationship and one that's toxic and that you need to remove from your life?

- ℰ We've all heard the saying "A little forgiveness goes a long way." How easy is it for you to forgive? to ask for forgiveness?

- ℰ How have you worked through conflicts in some of your most important relationships? What was successful? What didn't work?

Because *Real Women* Don't Need a *Cookbook*

French Twist

Sometimes for breakfast or just a fun treat, I slice a croissant in half and fill it with chocolate chips. I microwave this for about twenty seconds and voilà! Instant indulgence!

— Lisa in Nebraska

Seven Sweet Pick-Me-Ups

> When you need a quicker picker-upper, you can reach for a paper towel or some chocolate. Chocolate may taste better, but paper towels provide more dietary fiber. Tough choice, I know.

When we're traveling the rocky roads of life, sometimes we need endurance for the long haul ahead. Sometimes we need healing for whatever it is we've just come through. Sometimes we need compasses to make sense of the crazy terrain we have to negotiate.

But there are times when our biggest need is much more immediate, something to get us through the day. We need emotional pick-me-ups—kind of like a cup of coffee or handful of chocolate chips for the soul. Or maybe we just need a little support, like a Playtex bra for our spirits. (After all, some days our spirits long not only to be lifted but also separated from whatever hardships are present at the moment. Don't you agree?)

In other words, some days we simply need a quicker picker-upper, which I realize is the slogan for Bounty paper towels and not related to road trips or chocolate, but it feels appropriate nonetheless. And while paper towels don't taste nearly as good as chocolate chips, they have fewer calories and a lot more fiber.

For days like these, here is a list of seven sweet morsels—one a day for a full week—that will put an immediate lift in your step the next time you find yourself lagging. Or even if you aren't. A quick pick-me-up never hurts, so why not try all seven this week? Your life will definitely be a little sweeter as a result.

Monday's Sweet Morsel

Practice the one-word cure for grumpiness.

A couple of weeks ago, I woke up, thought about the day ahead of me, and groaned. Couldn't I just stay in bed instead?

Not that there was anything particularly horrible on my plate that day—just a mishmash of administrative tasks, loose ends, and errands. I found myself thinking stuff like this: *Let's see... I have to make that deposit. Oh, and I have to finish that report and get it to my clients. I have to put a roast in the oven, and I have to take my kids to buy shoes for school.*

I felt stressed! I was exhausted before my day even got started. Then I made a day-changing decision: I decided to make just one small change. And suddenly, my entire world seemed brighter.

The change I made was simple. In fact, it involved just one word. In my self-talk, I replaced the word *have* with the word *get*. With that, I had a whole new perspective on my day. I began thinking things like this:

- *Let's see... I get to make that deposit!*
- *Oh, and I get to finish that report and get it to my clients. (Thank God I have clients!)*

- *I get to put a roast in the oven, and I get to take my kids to buy shoes for school!*

Wow! Suddenly these tasks seemed more akin to opportunities than obligations. I went from feeling stressed to feeling blessed!

Try it. I know you'll like it.

Tuesday's Sweet Morsel

Finish something you've started.

You may have read in my book *Only Nuns Change Habits Overnight* about the ocean room and sea cave that Kacie and I created in her bedroom.[1] What you probably don't know is that even though Kacie and I finished building and painting the sea cave, we never did get around to painting any fish on the walls. Eventually, I showed the room to one of my friends, a very talented painter, and asked if she would help us add a sardine or two.

I think I'm a pretty creative person. Show me a boring turquoise room and I envision a sea cave. But my creativity pales to a color not unlike the underside of a jellyfish when compared to the energy and creativity that Stephanie Johnson brought to the project! More than one hundred hours later, Stephanie had repainted most of the room, adding elaborate stonework, a lifelike dolphin, coral, and sea life. Even an octopus, with six-foot-long tentacles. He's so realistic I hesitate to turn my back on him.

We added mood lighting on automatic sensors and a CD of waves crashing on a beach. The only thing I haven't found yet is seaweed-scented room spray. But believe me, I'm looking.

The project that Kacie and I started took several years to finish, but with Stephanie's help is now not only complete but pretty much the pièce de résistance of the entire house.[2]

I can't tell you how great it felt to finish what we started!

Obviously, Stephanie's investment of one hundred hours is way too much to fit into any given day. But my guess is that if you look around you'll find something that got left undone that you can complete in one day. And just think! Unlike Stephanie, you probably won't have to take Dramamine while you're doing it.

Wednesday's Sweet Morsel

Read *Alice in Wonderland* or *Through the Looking-Glass.* Out loud.

Trust me when I say that after reading the fantastical adventures of this spirited heroine—relayed in Lewis Carroll's witty writing— you'll be ready to adopt the plucky attitude you need to get you through your day. Alice's adventures, by the way, are best read aloud. And as you read, look for inspiring or whimsical nuggets to give you a new outlook or simply make you smile. Here are a few of my favorites:

> "There's no use trying," [Alice] said: "one can't believe impossible things."
>
> "I daresay you haven't had much practice," said the Queen. "When I was your age, I always did it for half-an-hour a day. Why, sometimes I've believed as many as six impossible things before breakfast."

> "Come, there's no use in crying like that!" said Alice to herself, rather sharply. "I advise you to leave off this minute!" She generally gave herself very good advice (though she very seldom followed it).

Consider what a great girl you are. Consider what a long way you've come to-day.

For, you see, so many out-of-the-way things had happened lately, that Alice had begun to think that very few things were really impossible.

"The horror of that moment," the King went on, "I shall never, never forget!" "You will, though," the Queen said, "if you don't make a memorandum of it."[3]

Thursday's Sweet Morsel

Get rid of clutter.

Organization is not my forte. I am not only chronically cluttered; I have posttraumatic stress disorder from being held hostage by my own coat closet and gadget drawers. If junk dealer Fred Sanford moved into my place, the first thing he'd do is get on the phone and call Merry Maids.

And yet even a junk-junkie like me knows there's something therapeutic about getting rid of clutter. When our personal worlds are tidied up a bit, we feel a little better—even if there's still chaos in the economy, in our careers, or even in our checking accounts.

Why is decluttering good therapy? For starters, taming our personal clutter puts us in control of at least part of our world, even when we can't get a grip on the other parts. Plus, a clutter-free environment creates a pleasant haven where we can retreat when life gets too stressful or uncertain. Getting organized also makes us more focused and productive. Just ask time-management guru Donald Wetmore, who reports that people with messy desks waste an average of ninety minutes a day digging through piles, looking for stuff they need.[4]

This morning, feeling a little overwhelmed with life, I went to the garage and dug around until I found my old Rolodex. Mind you, this Rolodex is not a little horizontal tray that holds business cards. It's the big carousel version that holds two-by-three-inch cards and spins them around in a rotisserie fashion, kind of like the chicken-roasting machine at your grocer's deli, except better because rotisserie chicken never saved anyone's life, at least that I know of.

This Rolodex, on the other hand, saved my life for an entire year.

I bought it several years ago and started using it to store all the phone numbers of friends, relatives, colleagues, associates, and anyone else I thought I might want to call one day. Then I added addresses. Then e-mail addresses. Then birthdays and passwords and the combination to my locker at the gym. Before long, I'd added the dates of my

Sweet Secrets

Q: What's your secret to a sweeter journey on the rocky road of life?

A: At the risk of sounding trite, I find that walking and praying changes everything. I usually ask God what I should learn from the situation. Almost always there's an answer to that.

—JONATHAN DAVID NEAL

last oil change, the name of the video game my kids wanted for Christmas, and the recipe for a homemade version of Play-Doh.

Soon I was going through my house with a laundry basket, collecting all the scraps of paper on which I'd written pertinent information. Like the shoe-box lid with the service ID number for my laptop. The table napkin with the birthdates of my nieces and nephews. The used envelope on which I'd written directions for programming my DVR.

After recording all this information on cards stuck in my Rolodex, I threw away the shoe-box lid, table napkin, and envelope. Then I started digging deeper, going through my wallet, sifting through piles on my desk. By now I was really on a roll! Dental appointment reminder cards. The brochure for the coming opera season that I never attend but always think I will. The salvaged magazine pages I'd hung on to for two years because they contained toll-free phone numbers for household gadgets I was almost sure I couldn't live without.

I recorded *everything* in my trusty Rolodex and tossed the clutter. In fact, this simple Rolodex kept my house clutter-free for an *entire year*, until the ill-fated day I decided to "upgrade" to a PDA.

A Rolodex is simple, straightforward, and self-explanatory. Any person who wants to use one can do so, with absolutely no training from an instructional DVD. You don't even need a pamphlet with diagrams. But all bets are off when you choose to upgrade (and I use the term ironically) to a PDA (the erroneously named Personal Digital Assistant). The word *assistant* clearly implies the device will be helpful. I, for one, was not assisted in the least.

After months of technical difficulties, software crashes, and an unending learning curve, I got frustrated. Worst of all, I reverted to my old ways, hanging on to random pieces of paper, writing things down on weird little scraps. Like rising floodwaters, clutter seeped and then poured back into my life. I've been drowning ever since.

At least until this morning, when I reclaimed my Old Friend from a box in the garage, right there next to the windshield-washer fluid.

I feel better already. Just *seeing* my old Rolodex gives me hope, because I know from experience that this simple office accouterment, this outdated data-storing widget, if you will, has the power to organize—no, *revolutionize*—my entire life. I'm not exaggerating.

Sweet Secrets

Q: What's your secret to a sweeter journey on the rocky road of life?

A: Besides brownies? :) When I'm having a really hard time and I can't pull myself out of a down place, I hunt for good, clean jokes or Christian joke sites on the Internet and force myself to read them, page after page, until at least three strike me as really funny. (I end up laughing at how lame the jokes are at first, then eventually my sense of humor kicks back in, and for some reason, if I can laugh, then I have a lot more hope.) P.S. The reason someone bought me one of your books in the first place was because of a season like that. :) Hugs to you!

—LISA-ANNE WOOLDRIDGE

I can't control the stock market. I can't control inflation or employee layoffs or currency fluctuations or the price of gold. Heck, for that matter, I can't even control my waistline. But thanks to my trusty Rolodex, I can get a handle on the sea of paper in my home.

See why unearthing this simple desktop gadget is such a big deal? It's not just a Rolodex. It's a way of life.

I'll bet you've never said that about a rotisserie chicken.

Friday's Sweet Morsel

Get acquainted with a random act of kindness.

Remember the random-acts-of-Starbucks-drive-through-kindness girl from chapter 1? All I can say is that this sweet morsel must really be working for Ronlyn, because after several months of whimsically picking up the tab for the customer behind her in the drive-through lanes of coffee shops and fast-food restaurants, she decided to take her good-deed addiction to a new level. Once a month, she and her son Hunter buy several dozen roses, tie a ribbon on each stem, then drive to a nursing home and pass out blooms to the women (and men) who live there.

They've been doing it now for about six months.

"And I never buy raggedy ones either!" Ronlyn told me. "I always look for the most beautiful roses I can find. Once I had to go to three stores. Sometimes I totally can't afford it, but I do it anyway. For some of these women and men, we may be the only visitors they see that month. Others can't remember the last time someone gave them flowers. That's why I love giving the best I can afford. I just hope it makes the people receiving the flowers feel even half as good as giving these roses makes *me* feel."

Saturday's Sweet Morsel

Say good-bye to toxins.

"A toxin is any element the body doesn't have a use for, like lead and mercury and hydrocarbons, and more mundane things like food colorings and hydrogenated fats," wrote Elson Haas, MD, author of *The Detox Diet* and founder of the Preventative Medical Center of Marin in San Rafael, California. "These toxins are in just about everything we come into contact with: polluted air and water, pesticides in foods, and chemicals in shampoos and medications. We store them in fat cells, in the brain and in the nervous system."[5]

Other toxins don't come from outside sources. They are, instead, products and by-products of our own bodies, and many are produced when we are stressed, angry, or depressed. For example, high levels of stress trigger the release of toxic amounts of brain chemicals called corticosteroids, which can cause permanent damage to brain cells.[6] Stress also triggers the release of adrenaline, which, in turn, increases the release of fat cells into the bloodstream. If the fat cells aren't used up by a burst of physical activity, they are turned into cholesterol.[7] Stress inspires our bodies to produce excess chemicals and hormones that can attack our brain cells, compromise our immune systems, endanger the health of our hearts, and more.[8]

In addition to biochemical toxins that are created as a result of our emotions, there are *thought toxins* as well. These are the negative thoughts and fallacies that we harbor that do us no earthly good. And I imagine if we are going to be thorough about this toxin thing, we can extend the concept to *time toxins*. What time wasters do we harbor that, if we were to be honest with ourselves, don't benefit us in any way?

One day this week, identify some of the toxins that may be hindering you from living the vibrant life you long for. Then get rid of them! Here are some toxin-reducing suggestions:

- Fast from junk food.
- Sweat, either by exercising or visiting a sauna. (Be sure to drink lots of filtered water to stave off dehydration.)
- Drink eight to ten glasses of filtered water.
- Eliminate a time waster from your day.
- Identify a lie you've been telling yourself and replace it with the truth.
- Consider any grudges—emotional toxins—you may be harboring in your life, and find one that you can toss out.
- Take a vacation from biochemical toxins by de-stressing your life.
- Give yourself a single day free from worry. If something you've been anxious about comes to mind, do as Scarlett O'Hara and promise yourself you'll think about it tomorrow.

Sunday's Sweet Morsel

Spend the day in What-If Land.

Spend one day entertaining the most delightful possibilities you can think of! If you're at a coffee shop and spot a woman reading a book, and a man using his laptop at another table, ask yourself, *What if they're both single and they leave the coffee shop at the same time and she drops her book and he picks it up for her, and then they look into each other's eyes and fall madly in love?*

If you see a rain cloud in the distance, ask yourself, *What if beneath that rain cloud there's a little girl who planted a garden in her backyard and for a week she has been praying that it will rain; and what if, when it starts to rain, she's going to believe for the first time that there really is a God who cares about her?*

If you reach into your pocket and realize you've lost the twenty you put there earlier that morning, ask yourself, *What if my money is found by a woman who's been out of work for a month and finally lands a job interview but doesn't have enough gas in her car to get there, and what if my twenty gets her to the interview where she receives a great job offer?*

And if you have a fight with a man you love, look deep into his eyes and ask yourself, *What if I stop letting myself be annoyed by the petty, stupid stuff this wonderful man does and start, instead, celebrating all the goofy, loving stuff he brings into my life?*

Try it for one day. You may never look at your world the same way again.

Food for Thought

- ✑ When you need an emotional pick-me-up, what works for you?
- ✑ Name one random act of kindness you could do today.
- ✑ Identify one thing you could do that would reduce the environmental toxins in your life. What about your diet, your chaotic schedule, your thoughts?
- ✑ If there's an unfinished project you've been meaning to get to, what has been stopping you? What do unfinished projects do to you emotionally? Are they energizing or draining? What impact would it have on your life if you devoted one day to wrapping up a lingering project?

Because *Real Women*
Don't Need a *Cookbook*

Raggedy Robins

If I don't have time for anything else, I get a soup spoon (not the wimpy-sized teaspoon), scrape a big blob of peanut butter out of the jar, then put a big blob of Nesquik on top of it, and depending on how stressed out I am, I either take tiny bites and savor it—or I down it all in one mouthful. (Of course, be careful not to inhale while you're doing this, or you'll choke on the Nesquik! Ask me how I know that!)

If I *do* have the time, I make a batch of Raggedy Robins and eat them until I'm sick. Even feeling sick, I feel better—at least until the food guilt sets in!

(This is a big recipe, so it can be halved.)

4 c. sugar

2 sticks butter

½ tsp. salt

1 c. milk

¾ c. cocoa

2 tsp. vanilla extract

1 ¾ c. peanut butter

6 c. Quick Quaker Oats

In a dutch oven, over medium heat, combine sugar, butter, salt, milk, and cocoa. Stir occasionally. Bring to *just* a boil, then remove from heat. Add

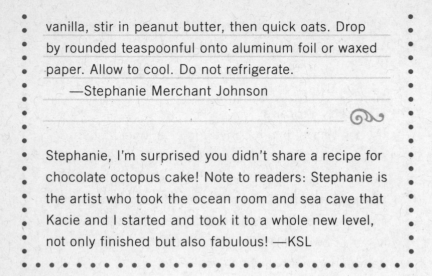

vanilla, stir in peanut butter, then quick oats. Drop by rounded teaspoonful onto aluminum foil or waxed paper. Allow to cool. Do not refrigerate.

—Stephanie Merchant Johnson

Stephanie, I'm surprised you didn't share a recipe for chocolate octopus cake! Note to readers: Stephanie is the artist who took the ocean room and sea cave that Kacie and I started and took it to a whole new level, not only finished but also fabulous! —KSL

There's More to Life Than Chocolate (Sometimes There's Chocolate with Nuts)

• • • • • • • •

If there is one thing that almost always helps when you're traveling on life's rocky roads, it's something nutty.

If you realize you need time to think, pray, and evaluate, it's best to go where you know you'll be alone. At those times you need privacy and freedom from distractions. But when you have to cope with life's rocky roads, it's better to travel with a friend.

A couple of years ago, I realized I needed to do something to bring in more regular monthly income. Being a writer and a speaker, I don't exactly get a consistent paycheck, which makes creating and maintaining a budget—what's the phrase? Oh, I remember now—a work of fiction.

So, two summers ago, I decided to turn a spare bedroom and bathroom into an efficiency apartment. I put up a few walls, added a kitchenette, exterior entrance, and even a cute little porch. This created a self-sufficient little apartment separate from the rest of my house. Still, as a single mom raising two daughters, I was a little nervous about advertising for a renter. (I decided to avoid placing ads on sites such as www.serialkillers.com.) As I went about trying to locate a reliable renter, I prayed, "God, please send us someone safe!"

On New Year's Day, a clean-cut man in his early thirties called in response to one of my ads. Bradley brought his girlfriend with him when he arrived to see the apartment. I liked them both right away, and he moved in three weeks later.

I told my kids, "This is a business relationship, not a friendship."

Kacie said, "Can't we invite him over to watch a movie?"

I said, "No."

My nephew Isaac said, "Can he come over for Ping-Pong?"

I said, "No."

They said, "Pizza?"

I said, "No."

Two months later Bradley and his girlfriend broke up. He seemed a little lost, so we invited him over to watch a movie. The kids talked him into a game of Ping-Pong. I think we probably even ordered pizza.

Over the following months, as I grew to know and trust Bradley, I realized God had brought us more than a renter. He'd brought us a friend. Maybe even a long-lost relative, as Bradley became a goofy uncle for the kids, a brother to me.

Bradley and I spent many evenings drinking coffee and talking. We shared stories about God and his impact on our lives. We analyzed our relationships with people we were dating. We brainstormed ways to improve our finances. Sometimes we even talked about various hurts we'd suffered or stupid things we'd done in the past, and how to forgive ourselves and move on. Sometimes, if I had to spend the evening writing or working, Bradley kept me company, sitting at the kitchen table and playing FarmVille on Facebook.[1]

One day, I was upset. I'd just gotten a call from my dermatologist with lab results on a flaky patch of skin below my left eye. The good news was that the patch wasn't melanoma, but garden-variety basal cell skin cancer. The bad news was that removing it could prove interesting, being so close to my tear duct and all.

Bradley was playing FarmVille when I told him the news. He cut to the chase. "So what's your worst fear?" he asked.

My first thought was, *Gee, can't you come up with something a little more positive?* But I didn't say that. I pondered his question, then said, "Disfigurement."

Bradley didn't respond. He simply continued playing FarmVille. A few minutes later, his eyes still glued to the screen, he said simply, "Whew. Disfigurement. That's a tough one."

Suddenly we were both laughing, and I realized something. Bradley's question was the right one after all. Because suddenly there was nothing lurking unsaid in the shadows. My worst fear was on the table for both of us to look at. And guess what? We were still laughing. In fact, at that very moment, Bradley harvested a pumpkin and bought a cow.

I felt better already.

Make Friends. Live Well.

The benefits of connection are undeniable. The therapy you get from talking through everyday problems with a friend can ward off more serious problems, like depression or insomnia (or even obesity for those of us who turn to food to deal with stress or sadness). According to research, "What you get when you don't release your feelings on a regular basis is a balloon-like effect where stress builds up and blood pressure rises, eventually triggering a number of negative consequences, including moodiness and poor sleep. The toll it can take on you physically could end up being far worse than your initial worries."[2]

If you have a large network of friends, your risk of a heart attack goes down. And if you hang out with lots of friends, you have a better chance of staying healthy during cold and flu season (despite the fact that spending time with people actually increases your exposure to viruses!).

Connection does more than prevent illness—it can also be healing. Even more impressive, it may actually extend your life! An article in the *New York Times* revealed these startling results: "In 2006, a study of nearly 3,000 nurses with breast cancer found that women without close friends were four times as likely to die from the disease as women with 10 or more friends."[3] Another landmark study—this one by Stanford University in 1989—showed that "women with breast cancer who took part in social activities suffered much less pain and went on to live twice as long as those" who were less active with their friends.[4] And finally, following a decade-long study of fifteen hundred elderly people, the Center for Aging Studies at Flinders University in Australia revealed that those who had a large network of friends tended to live longer by about twenty-two percent than those who had the least number of friends.[5]

The Doctor Is...Awake

Being there for my friends and family is one of my sweetest joys. Even getting a good night's sleep pales in comparison to the satisfaction of being there for the people I love.

One night my cell phone gave three short chirps, waking me from a dead sleep. Who was texting at this hour? I suspected it might be my sister Michelle, who was working nights as a police dispatcher, or my daughter Kaitlyn, a college student.

"R u sleeping?" It was Michelle.

I typed, "Depends what you mean by sleeping. If you mean that unconscious-REM-phase thing, yeah, I was sleeping. Are you okay?"

Michelle wrote, "Kinda down. But go back to sleep. We'll talk tomorrow."

I replied, "Look, if it's about men, everything's going to be okay. Sure, we may be single right now, but we're strong and beautiful women and we'll be fine. Cross me heart." Noticing the typo, I added, "When did I turn into a pirate?" and hit Send.

Immediately my phone chirped again. This time it was a text from Kaitlyn! She wrote: "I hate my life. A coffee shop charged two HUNDRED dollars on my debit card instead of TWO dollars, and four checks bounced. I need to call the bank, but I'm so overwhelmed I can't even make the call."

I wrote back, "Sometimes we have to find our strong inner cores

Sweet Secrets

Q: What's your secret to a sweeter journey on the rocky road of life?

A: Drink an iced caramel latte on warm days or a Caramel Macchiato on cold days.

—JENNIFER CHUMBLEY

and rise to the occasion and do the thing we think we cannot do, but really can."

I looked for a reply from Michelle on my pirate quip. Nothing. I texted: "Stop saving lives and answer me."

She keyed back, "Sorry. Just sending units rolling on an ax-murderer, terrorist-sniper call. No biggie. What were you saying?"

By now Kaitlyn had written, "I'll try."

I fired off a series of texts reminding Kaitlyn that in the middle of the night, it's easy to let fears and worries eclipse hope and reason. I encouraged her to separate the task at hand from any feelings of inadequacy or anxiety and simply dial the phone and get it done. I assured her she could handle this simple phone call with one hand tied behind her back (unless, of course, it was her dialing hand).

Texting Michelle, I wrote: "Things could be worse. I was at the tire store today with Dad, and we couldn't tell if the clerk was a man or woman. Even the name tag didn't help. It said *Jess.* Just as I concluded Jess was a woman, Dad blurted, 'You're a fine young man. You'll go far in this business.' Which is why you and I need to cheer up. We may not be dating men right now, but at least no one thinks we're men."

In the middle of all this texting, I wondered why psychologists and life coaches don't offer night hours. Then again, if therapists had night hours, I guess the rest of us wouldn't get to pick up the slack and encourage one another. People I love have certainly been there to assuage *my* midnight fears. I considered myself blessed to be there for Michelle and Kaitlyn.

Texting Michelle, I assured her there is a male who adores us and would love to take us for moonlit strolls in the park, even if he does wear a rabies tag and licks his own fur.

Then I texted Kaitlyn: "I must be getting tired. I just told your aunt that Buddy would make a good date..."

Suddenly it dawned on me that I hadn't gotten any texts in a while. I texted Michelle. "Where are you?"

She wrote, "My break ended half an hour ago. Can't text. Go to bed. Luv u."

I dialed Kaitlyn. She answered on the fourth ring, sounding groggy. I said, "Are you *sleeping?*"

"Yeah. I went to bed. Can we talk tomorrow, Mom? I'm beat. Besides, do you know what time it is?"

We hung up.

I blinked at my phone for several minutes before putting it on the nightstand. I rolled over and closed my eyes. I adjusted my pillow. I opened my eyes. I stared at the ceiling. I adjusted my pillow again.

Do I know what time it is? You bet I do. Time to start posting office hours.

Even Midnight Therapists Need Love

As I said, I love being there for my family and friends. But sometimes even midnight therapists need some serious handholding. This was the case with me last year.

I knew I was stressed because my kitchen was filled with sawdust. Sometimes when I'm stressed I select a perfectly good wall in my house and tear it down. I don't know why. Stress must release some sort of remodeling hormone into my bloodstream, because I can't seem to help myself. When I'm stressed, I reach for the Sawzall and usually have to call a repairman in the morning.

This time, when one of my girlfriends told me she was looking for a room to rent, I got to thinking. With a little remodeling, I could rent her a large bedroom on the main floor of my house. This was perfect! I could distract myself from the stress in my life with lots of hammering and dry-wall dust, generate a little more monthly income, *and* add another member to the cast of quirky characters living in my household (which already included Bradley, Kacie, me, and even Kaitlyn in recurring cameos as the adult daughter who pops in weekly for advice and chocolate).

There simply wasn't a downside. I forged ahead with my plan, and Mame moved in after Christmas.

After the sawdust settled I realized it was time to stop distracting myself and face some major sadness and stressors in my life. There were money stressors, to be sure. But they were only a portion of the burden I'd been carrying. There was something else, a generalized sadness I couldn't quite bear to look at.

The best I could tell, I very much missed "K," a man I'd dated for six months until we both realized the timing of our relationship was disastrous. Plus, I suspected I still had a little healing to do from my breakup four years earlier with Skippy. (You may remember reading about him in previous books I've written.)

The longer I looked at the sadness, the more I began to think it predated these broken relationships. One night I was rereading my

· · · · ❧ *Sweet Secrets* ☙ · · · ·

Q: What's your secret to a sweeter journey on the rocky road of life?

A: You are writing about two of my favorite topics: chocolate and coping with grace! I've had a love affair with chocolate since childhood—the darker the chocolate the better. It's as if I can feel it coursing through my veins. And I have to say, this year was a banner chocolate year.

First, I lost my mom. Shortly afterward, my dad was stricken by a severe neurological disorder, I had my first car wreck, and my only daughter got married and moved out of state. I had two new bosses, and my grandson was born prematurely. All of this happened within eight months.

I have secret stashes of chocolate in my office, semisweet chocolate chips in the cabinet, dark chocolate ice cream in the deep freeze, and if I get a stepladder, I can almost reach my husband's stash of chocolate mint Girl Scout cookies. My favorite stress relief is to grab a bowl of dutch chocolate Blue Bell ice cream, march chocolate mint Girl Scout cookies around the edge of the bowl, douse with chocolate syrup, and sprinkle chocolate-covered coffee beans on top. While I enjoy eating this on the couch, it is best enjoyed in my hammock chair under the mulberry tree with one of Mom's letters.

The combination of chocolate, Mom's handwritten verses, the lazy swirl of the hammock, and the deepening Texas sunset reminds me that my life really is blessed.

—BONNIE, DUNCANVILLE, TEXAS

journal and noticed the strangest thing. Here and there—inserted randomly into paragraphs about work, kids, friends, and even finances—I kept finding a single sentence. It rarely had anything to do with the topic on the page where it was scrawled, but there it would be. It was a disconnected thought, inked into my journal as darkly as it had, apparently, been inscribed on my soul. The seemingly random phrase was this: *I don't know why my husband didn't love me.*

One night I called one of my sisters. I told her about my journal. I told her about trying to stay afloat financially. I told her about feeling weary and overwhelmed. "I can't even muster the energy I need to do the things that would help me get ahead," I confessed. "I need to call a lawyer to recalculate child support, but I can't do that until I get caught up on tax returns. And I can't file my taxes until I sort through about a year's worth of mail I've been collecting in baskets in my office. And until I sort through all my paperwork and get the taxes filed, I can't finish applying for the refinance that would lower my mortgage payments. I feel so overwhelmed I don't even know where to start!"

And I began to cry.

Michelle said, "I don't know what to do about the journal, or the sadness, but I can help you with the rest. Karen, you don't know where to start, but I do. Bring all your baskets of mail to my house tomorrow."

When Mame heard the plan, she offered to help as well. Together, Mame and I took several big baskets of mail and paperwork to Michelle's. We began to open and sort, organizing everything into smaller piles all over the floor, coffee table, and even the top of the piano. Michelle's eleven-year-old daughter, Gigi, joined us for a while. Four hours later we were done. Four hours! To get the job done, it took twelve woman-hours plus girl-sized assistance.

And that was just to open my mail. Now the real work could begin.

Hope Is a Curious Thing

Over the next four months, I worked on tax returns and loan documents. I photocopied bank statements. I learned how to create profit-and-loss statements for my businesses. Some days it felt as if I would never dig out of the hole I'd fallen into. Michelle and Mame had gotten me moving. Without their help I'd still be clinging, paralyzed, to a narrow ledge a fair distance down the side of a bottomless well. Now I was climbing out, one toehold at a time, but between the work ahead of me and the sadness inside me, I often felt weary beyond words. I remember one night, sitting with my parents in a booth at Rosie's Diner, crying from sheer weariness and a hint of despair. They talked with me for hours. I recall little of what was said, but I do remember the hazy sense that within their words ran delicate strands of hope and that somewhere in the murky darkness below me, these strands were crisscrossing into a fragile net.

During this time someone else came alongside me. John Koiter and I had been acquaintances for months, but about the time Michelle, Mame, Gigi, and I started tackling my baskets of mail, John began showing up regularly. Sometimes we went to dinner. Sometimes we window-shopped at the mall. Sometimes we grilled hamburgers at his house or made tacos at mine. He and Kacie enjoyed conversations both serious and goofy. He talked about missions trips with Kaitlyn and bantered with Mame and Bradley.

When I discovered a water leak beneath my kitchen sink, John installed a new faucet the next day. A piano tuner by trade, he tuned my piano several times. When I decided to start jogging, he researched the best running shoes for my particular gait, took me shopping, and didn't let me pay him for the shoes.

Sometimes John and I asked ourselves if we were dating, but most of the time we pretty much agreed that we probably weren't. We didn't know what the future held for our friendship, but for the time being we agreed that it was an important connection.

Later, John—who had been divorced two years when we met—would say that our friendship helped him heal from the demise of his thirty-year marriage. He would tell me that spending time with the quirky collage of humanity living at my house helped him transition out of the cocoon he'd been in, rekindled his confidence, and encouraged him to wake up and start to really live again.

As for me, I was trying to rebuild my life in almost every area, and it became increasingly clear to me that John (and Mame, Bradley, my family, and others) were God's gift to me during an incredibly difficult season of healing and rebuilding. With John I felt supported in a non-dependent way. We weren't a couple, so transferring my problems onto John's shoulders wasn't an option. I had to keep rescuing myself, but he gave me the courage and confidence to do it.

One day I posted on Facebook, "Karen Linamen feels a little bit hopeful." Numerous people commented, including John, who wrote: "Hope is a curious thing. It keeps us in the game until the momentum turns. A little is plenty."

I printed out his words and posted them on my fridge.

Too Much of a Very Good Thing?

Our traveling companions on the journey of life can be a source of strength and hope and even healing. But have you ever found yourself in a relationship with someone who—despite very good intentions—is actually holding you back from where you need to go?

Kris Harty was seven years old when she was diagnosed with juvenile rheumatoid arthritis. Forty years and eight surgeries later, Kris is mobile with the help of a walking stick. She told me, "By nature of my outward appearance, I attract people who want to help. The risk is that I can also attract people who want to help for the wrong reasons. They need me to stay in a role of a 'lesser, needier' person so they can feel good about themselves."

The healthiest friendships, Kris said, blossom between people who don't have to leverage the other person's weakness to feel better about themselves, but between people who can recognize and celebrate one another's strengths and successes.

It's a risk of relationship, to be sure. But Kris believes it's a risk worth taking.

"People in my life have been a real blessing—I couldn't have accomplished the things I've accomplished without the help of friends along the way. Together, we help one another reach places and heights we could never have reached alone."

Today Kris is an inspirational speaker, author, and thought leader on people helping people persevere. She writes a weekly column for nurses and other health-care providers, and is the president of Strong Spirit Unlimited. She's been on the receiving end of help and encouragement, and she knows how to be on the giving end as well.[6]

As we travel the rocky road of life, it's easy to feel isolated and alone. And yet, we have the privilege of receiving—and giving!—hope, help, and healing when we make the journey side by side.

Ecclesiastes 4:12 (NLT) says it well: "A person standing alone can be attacked and defeated, but two can stand back-to-back and conquer. Three are even better, for a triple-braided cord is not easily broken." We don't have to solve one another's problems. In fact, most of the time we could never fix the dilemmas in the lives of those we love, even if we tried. But that doesn't mean what we *can* provide for one another is without value.

Sometimes a glimpse of hope, a new pair of running shoes, or a repaired leak in the kitchen is just what the doctor ordered.

Food for Thought

According to Kris Harty, discerning the right people to lean on when there's something you can't do on your own takes time and practice. She said, "If you make a mistake, don't beat yourself up. Just learn from the experience. Ask yourself, 'Was that the best person to lean on, and, if not, how can I make a better choice in the future?'"

- Do you think it's possible to lean too heavily on someone? If so, what are some signs of that? How do you keep "helping relationships" healthy?

- If you're traveling a bumpy road and there's not a friend in sight, how can you cope in the meantime?

- Think about a time when the right person or people showed up just when you needed them most. Have you ever been that person for someone else?

- When someone you know is traveling a rocky road and you have the opportunity to help or encourage that person, do you know when to stop helping? Are you as passionate about recognizing and celebrating your friends' strengths and victories as you are about compensating for their weaknesses?

Because *Real Women*
Don't Need a *Cookbook*

Chocolate on Chocolate Trifle

1 pkg. (18¼ oz.) chocolate fudge cake mix
1 pkg. (6 oz.) instant chocolate pudding mix
½ c. strong black coffee (the morning
    java-jolt kind)
1 carton (12 oz.) frozen whipped topping,
    thawed
6 Heath bars (1.4 oz. each), crushed, or
    another hard crunchy chocolate bar of
    your choice

Bake cake according to directions, then cool.
Prepare pudding mix according to package instruc-
tions and set aside. Crumble the cake; set a half cup
of it aside. Place half the cake crumbs in the bottom
of a trifle bowl, layer with half of the coffee, half of the
pudding, half of the whipped topping, and half of the
crushed candy bars. Repeat the layers of cake, coffee,
pudding, and whipped topping. Mix the remaining
crushed candy bars with the set-aside cake crumbs
and sprinkle on top. Refrigerate for four hours, or if
desperate, get four spoons and call some girlfriends.
—Bonnie, Duncanville, Texas

Eat Chocolate. Write More. Feel Better.

For twenty years researchers have been stumbling onto the same findings: writing is good medicine.

Justus von Liebig, a German chemist, once wrote: "Chocolate is a perfect food, as wholesome as it is delicious, a beneficent restorer of exhausted power. It is the best friend of those engaged in literary pursuits."[1]

As a renowned nineteenth-century scientist, Liebig was qualified to identify the perfect food. As an avowed chocoholic, I've done plenty of research to verify his findings. And as someone engaged in literary pursuits, I figure if anyone is entitled to follow his advice about making chocolate their best friend, it's me. In fact, not twenty minutes ago as I was heading toward my office, my friend Mame said, "You're going to write? Then you'll need chocolate for strength." And she gave me some.

Perhaps you're thinking, *But what's* my *excuse for eating chocolate?*

I'm not a writer! To which I can only reply, "Ah, but if I have anything to do with it, my friend, you'll be a writer before you finish reading this chapter."

Top Ten Reasons to Become a Writer

10. Financial security and cash flow are overrated.
9. You can wear a bathrobe while you work.
8. Friends never ask you if they can borrow money.
7. The antacid industry sends you thank-you gifts.
6. You get to tell yourself that the next time your phone rings it could be Oprah's Book Club.
5. You can dress like Jack Klugman when you're working.
4. When you text your friends, it still looks like English.
3. You can wear a ninja cape when you work.
2. Finding typos in prnt gives you a rush.
1. And the number one reason to become a writer: You'll be healthier, with fewer colds, lower blood pressure, and a stronger immune system. You'll just be plain ol' happier too.

Write for the Health of Your Body and Your Emotions

Myriad benefits can be yours when you take pen in hand. For starters, writing can make you healthier in your body and in your emotions. For real.

Of course, not every kind of writing makes you healthier and happier. Writing about time management, for example, won't necessarily do the trick. But journaling about events that have caused emotional upheavals in your life—especially if you write about how these events impacted your future, your relationships, your career, and so on—is another story altogether.

Researchers asked a group of people to spend three days writing about emotional events and drawing correlations between those events and other areas of their lives. They asked a second group to spend three days writing on nonemotional subjects such as time management. As researchers followed both groups over time, they discovered that the folks who had journaled about emotional events reported fewer illnesses, went to see a doctor less often, and showed fewer symptoms of afflictions like depression and even asthma.

How Does This Work?

When you and I are surprised by painful events—trauma, illness, abuse, violence, or loss—we often think such events are senseless and random. In the puzzle of life, they can feel like pieces that don't fit. They're twists of a plot without a story, and that bothers us (and rightfully so!) because story lines give not only context and meaning but boundaries and even rules.

Because our minds are most settled when things make sense, our thoughts return often to the fragments of painful memories and emotions, searching for a story. Little things remind us constantly of the trauma we experienced as our brains keep returning to the rogue puzzle pieces, trying to figure out where they belong in the big picture of our lives.

Yet even as we long for context and meaning, we also hate pain. And because these fragmented puzzle pieces are tied to painful events, it's tempting to avoid thinking about them deeply enough to assign the meaning we so desperately crave.

What happens next is that you and I can spend years—even lifetimes—both avoiding and being haunted by painful fragments of memories and emotions. Eventually they create havoc with our emotional wellness, our relationships, and even our health. As we know, emotional stress accounts for ninety percent of all doctors' visits. In the words of one marriage and family counselor, "Emotions left unattended can change into symptoms that cause confusion when they present in physicians' offices."

Belonging nowhere, these painful memories and emotions surface everywhere. According to Dr. James Pennebaker and Janel Seagal, authors of *Writing to Heal,* when we journal about these events, the narrative we create helps anchor the trauma securely within a context of the bigger story of our lives. In other words, we take the floating puzzle pieces and find permanent places for them in the bigger picture of our lives. Plus, making a coherent story out of events that feel messy or chaotic helps us feel more in control. Finally, we feel more peaceful because placing our traumas within the larger context of our stories allows our brains to stop striving to make sense of painful experiences.[2]

Can all this peace and well-being translate into fewer stress-related

❧ Sweet Secrets ❧

Q: What's your secret to a sweeter journey on the rocky road of life?

A: Prayer works. So does talking to friends. Music also works well!

—CHRIS ALBRACHT, AMARILLO, TEXAS

and emotion-related maladies? You bet. People who have followed Pennebaker's writing guidelines have seen results in terms of lower blood pressure, stronger immune systems, decrease in symptoms of depression, improved grades, improved performance at sports, fewer days absent from work or school, and more. These benefits have been proven to last months and even years.

Want to give it a try? Here's what Dr. Pennebaker prescribed:

> For the next four days, I would like for you to write about your very deepest thoughts and feelings about the most traumatic experience of your entire life. In your writing, I'd like you to really let go and explore your very deepest emotions and thoughts. You might tie your topic to your relationships with others, including parents, lovers, friends, or relatives, to your past, your present, or your future, or to who you have been, who you would like to be, or who you are now. You may write about the same general issues or experiences on all days of writing or on different traumas each day. All of your writing will be completely confidential.[3]

You may choose to share your writing with others, or you may choose not to. It's up to you. The benefits of journaling don't seem to wax or wane depending on whether your writing is shared, published, or kept private. Studies indicate that the important thing is the writing process itself, not what happens to your story after it's written.

Write to Manage Transitions in Your Life

Writing makes us healthier and helps us cope. It can also help us negotiate the tumultuous waters of major change in our lives.

Chuck Maher is a certified financial planner in Colorado Springs. He specializes in morally responsible portfolios that perform competitively without including companies that support abortion or pornography. He also co-leads—with an attorney and a psychologist—workshops to help women manage the legal, emotional, and financial implications of divorce. According to Maher, all three instructors (the lawyer, the mental health professional, and the financial planner) advise women to do the same thing: *keep a journal.*

I think this is fascinating.

Each instructor has a different reason for giving this advice, to be

❧ Sweet Secrets ❧

Q: What's your secret to a sweeter journey on the rocky road of life?

A: Read a good book. Of course, the Bible is the best. But sometimes I venture to the wild side and read funny books by the gorgeous author named Karen Linamen! ;>) So glad I saw your books at the Christian bookstore several years ago. My husband kept asking me, "What is so funny?" Thanks for reminding me of my ultimate Source of comfort. "Taste and see that the Lord is good; blessed is the man who takes refuge in him" (Psalm 34:8).

—Nanette Schow

sure. But the bottom line is the same—write, write, write!—and underscores the importance of this seemingly mundane assignment.

The psychologist advises women to keep a daily journal because writing helps them cope with all the emotional upheaval. The lawyer encourages clients to keep a journal because, as Maher explains, "The person with the best records has the most credibility in the courtroom. When you're down to 'he says, she says' and you have a whole list of dates and times, your records are more credible."[4]

As a financial planner, Maher recommends journaling as a way of managing not only emotions but also the details, tasks, and strategies that will make a difficult transition go more smoothly. He says journaling can help a woman feel calmer during a chaotic process, and a journal is also a place to keep track of things in order to protect herself financially.

"A woman facing divorce has a lot on her plate," he explains. "She may carry the bigger burden in many respects. In all likelihood, she's going to retain the lion's share of custody of their children, so she's figuring out how she's going to take care of her kids. If she hasn't been the primary breadwinner, the thought of losing income or trying to jump-start a career can generate a lot of fear. Men are hunters, always moving forward, looking for what's ahead on the track; women aren't hunters, women are caregivers, and a woman may not be used to taking the time to care for herself, or setting up support systems she needs. And all this is happening during a time when she needs to be financially savvy, to remember details, and to take specific actions that can help protect her assets and give her greater financial stability after the divorce. Journaling can help her manage all this."[5]

While Maher and his colleagues prescribe writing for women facing divorce, their reminder that journaling is good for coping, remembering things, and managing emotions or tasks applies to all of us.

There simply isn't a good reason *not* to enjoy the benefits of journaling every day, whether we are navigating paths of change in our lives or just figuring out how to get through a hectic day.

Write to Feel Known

Writing helps us feel better emotionally and physically. It helps us use narrative to anchor past trauma securely to a previous chapter in our lives so we can move forward. Writing helps us manage transitions. Finally, writing helps us feel known. Author Matthew Kelly wrote, "The sensation that nobody really knows us can be one of the most debilitating forms of loneliness."[6]

My friend Emily felt that way growing up. She was born the youngest of six kids and grew up with a couple of abusive brothers, an abusive father, and a mother who was always sick. She told me, "I remember living with the fear that my mother was going to die. I would wake up in the middle of the night to hear her falling; she would get up to go to the bathroom, walk down the hall, and fall. I never knew what was wrong with her."

When Emily cried or talked about her fears, her brothers would tease her mercilessly and call her a baby. Even if she laughed, she risked a beating. "You know those laughing attacks that kids sometimes get? You're sitting at the dinner table and something strikes you as funny and you can't stop laughing? Sometimes my dad would let us get away with it. Other times he would completely lose it, screaming at us to stop laughing and, if we didn't, he'd take us into the next room and beat us with his belt, yelling, 'I'll teach you what's so funny...'"

The best way to survive her childhood, Emily said, was to become as invisible as possible. No tears. No laughing. No voice.

"Journaling gave me a voice," she said. "It was the only place I was allowed to express my feelings. I journaled to know myself, to figure how I felt about things and why. I also journaled so I could feel known."

Emily added, "Maybe I was a melodramatic kid, but I remember thinking, *If I die, someone will find this and read this and know what I went through.* But even if my words were never discovered, it still helped. I wrote to feel 'heard' even if I wasn't audibly heard. Even if you never show your writing to anyone, there's the sense that God hears you."[7]

Her words reminded me of Mathew Kelly's observation that "Within each of us there is a story that wants to be told. Intimacy means sharing our story."[8]

When Emily was just fifteen, her oldest sister, Susie, was murdered by her ex-husband. Emily's childhood fantasy of having people know her by reading her journals after her death took a tragic twist in real life when Emily read her sister's diary. Emily said, "Reading Susie's diary after she died was eye opening. I found out she was pregnant when she married at nineteen, which was the reason she married so quickly. I could also see from her diary that she really did love her husband, which was scary, knowing how it all ended. I was just a kid when Susie married, not much older when she divorced, and was just fifteen when she died. Reading her story in her own words was a gift to me, giving me the chance to know and understand her in a way I never would have had the chance to do if she hadn't put her story onto the written page."[9]

"Write Two Pages and Call Me in the Morning"

I've yet to hear those words from a doctor. (From my editor, sure, but never from a doctor!) And yet writing really is good medicine. Better yet, it really can help us make sense of the sometimes disorienting combination of ingredients we've been given to work with in our lives.

So go ahead. Be a writer. Do it for your health. Do it to help manage stress in your life. Do it to feel known. And if that's not reason enough to take pen in hand, you can always heed the immortal words of Justus von Liebig and do it for the chocolate.

Food for Thought

- ✍ Try James Pennebaker's assignment for three days. How did it make you feel? Did you share your writing with someone else or choose to keep it private?

- ✍ What types of writing have you tried? Journaling, poetry, fiction, nonfiction, songwriting—something else? If you have not given it a try, what do you think is keeping you from putting pen to paper (or fingertips to keyboard)?

- ✍ Journaling can help to anchor the trauma in your life, to help you feel more in control of life's messiness, and to help you see your story—your life—in context. If you have begun journaling your thoughts, has doing so helped you to release your emotional pain?

- ✍ In order to survive her traumatic childhood, Emily said, "Journaling gave me a voice." Has writing given a voice to your pain—enabling you to finally feel that you are being heard?

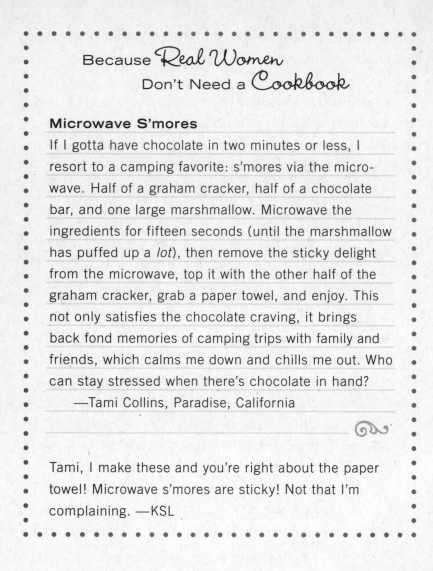

Because *Real Women*
Don't Need a *Cookbook*

Microwave S'mores

If I gotta have chocolate in two minutes or less, I resort to a camping favorite: s'mores via the micro-wave. Half of a graham cracker, half of a chocolate bar, and one large marshmallow. Microwave the ingredients for fifteen seconds (until the marshmallow has puffed up a *lot*), then remove the sticky delight from the microwave, top it with the other half of the graham cracker, grab a paper towel, and enjoy. This not only satisfies the chocolate craving, it brings back fond memories of camping trips with family and friends, which calms me down and chills me out. Who can stay stressed when there's chocolate in hand?

—Tami Collins, Paradise, California

Tami, I make these and you're right about the paper towel! Microwave s'mores are sticky! Not that I'm complaining. —KSL

Inner Children Need Chocolate Too (and Maybe Some Ducks)

Life includes everyday recipes that help you stay young at heart.

Yesterday a few of my friends were talking about the importance of staying young in spirit. Mame piped up and said, "Karen's such a big kid, the only way her daughters can rebel is to act responsible and grown up."

She had a point. When Kaitlyn was a freshman in college, my father told her, "I'm always glad when you're back home on breaks and weekends. Then I know there's at least *one* grownup in your house."

It's good to be childlike.

Life is demanding, even on our best days. On our less-than-best days, it's overwhelming, exhausting, and nerve-racking. I figure when that happens, we've got a couple of options. We can reach for the Rolaids, or we can suck the air from a helium balloon and talk like ducks. Either way, we'll feel better. But if we talk like ducks, everyone within hearing range will feel better too.

Sometimes when I'm facing life's challenges, I ask my inner child what she would do in my situation. I've gotten a lot of great advice this way. Here are a few of the things I've learned:

- To get bubblegum out of your hair, use peanut butter. To get peanut butter out of your hair, use a puppy.
- You can't hide a piece of broccoli in a glass of milk.
- Never hold a DustBuster and a cat at the same time.
- Sometimes crying helps. Crying on someone's shoulder *always* helps.
- Barbie night-lights aren't just for kids.
- The next time you need to eat an entire box of cereal in a single sitting, pick something other than Cap'n Crunch. (With the Cap'n, you won't like what happens to the roof of your mouth.)
- Chocolate milk and a nap can fix almost anything.

Take Three Ducks and Call Me in the Morning

In addition to gaining valuable insights from my inner child, sometimes I learn things from the inner children of my closest friends. Like, for example, Ilene.

I hadn't seen my friend Ilene in months. She came over recently, bearing fresh eggs from her ranch. We made omelets, drank coffee, and caught up on each other's lives.

Ilene said, "We have ducks now."

Ilene and Tom raise chickens for eggs. They graze cattle for money. They raise barn cats for mousing. I said, "Ducks? What can ducks do?"

"Nothing," she grinned. "The ducks are for fun. It's been a stressful year, and Tom thought I needed ducks. I told him ducks are a lot of work. He said, 'I'll help you.' I reminded him that this winter the wading pool will be frozen, and we'll have to schlep fresh water to them every morning. He said, 'I'll do it.' I said I didn't want to add more work to everything else he already does around the place."

"And what did he say?" I had to know.

Imitating Tom's voice, she said firmly, *"Ilene, let me help you have ducks."*

I thought it was a strange offer until I spent fifteen minutes watching Ilene laugh, quack, and waddle around my kitchen illustrating the antics of her comical pets. Except I wasn't just watching, I was laughing too. In fact, we were still laughing over Ilene's ducks—named, by the way, after her father's three sisters—when Ilene left my house. She may have named them after her aunties, but with the kind of benefits she's getting from her feathered therapists, I think she should have named them Frasier, Freud, and Dr. Phil.

"I Didn't Make That Noise. No, Really."

I recently met another inner child, the one that inspires my friend Cynthia. Cynthia's daughter Rachel, however, thinks Little Cynthia is a troublemaker. Rachel is a teen model. One morning she had a modeling gig at a local television station. Rachel was standing in the station's break room with other models, makeup artists, cameramen, and producers, holding her mother's purse while Cynthia visited the ladies' room. All of a sudden, the unmistakable sound of human gas trumpeted through the break room. All eyes turned to fourteen-year-old Rachel.

Rachel stammered, "That wasn't me."

No one said a word.

The sound of yet another gastrointestinal emission—this one longer and louder than the first—filled the air.

"I'm serious," Rachel said urgently. "It's coming from my mom's purse."

No one believed her until she opened the purse and pulled out a small practical joke soundbox. "It's one of my mom's toys." Apparently, while Rachel was holding her mom's purse, someone had called Cynthia, and her vibrating cell phone had triggered the device.

When Cynthia and Rachel told me this story, they were laughing hysterically. Okay, Cynthia was laughing. Rachel looked mortified. I'd love to tell you why Cynthia carries around a toy that toots, but I didn't even ask. This is because *why* she carries it doesn't matter. The only thing that matters is that she does.

Whistling in the Dark

In the last chapter I shared the story of Emily who, as a child, discovered journaling as a way to cope with hardship. For her, journaling remains a tool she uses to sweeten her life. She also writes poetry and shares her work at poetry-reading events around town.

Journaling isn't the only secret to a sweeter journey that can follow us from childhood into adulthood. Another of Emily's childhood secrets, for example, is singing. This has helped her cope since she was little.

"I was maybe seven," she said, "and I would go outside, sit on our backyard swing set, and sing. Sometimes I'd make up songs, but most often I'd sing hymns or spirituals I'd heard at church. It was very comforting."

You may remember Emily's story. The youngest of six kids, Emily grew up with two abusive brothers, an abusive dad, and a mom who was always ill. Emily felt like the only way to stay safe was to make herself as invisible as possible. Journaling gave her a voice and helped her feel known, if only to herself and God. Apparently music gave her a voice too.

She said, "I remember singing negro spirituals. They have so much sadness in them, but some of the songs have a lot of hope too." At this, she paused and began to sing. The image she had painted for me was of a seven-year-old sitting on a swing, twirling from side to side as the swing chains twist and untwist, and singing just to hear the comforting sound of her own voice.[1] But Emily isn't seven anymore; her voice is grownup and soulful and as rich as chocolate. Still, she sings with a

❧ Sweet Secrets ❧

Q: What's your secret to a sweeter journey on the rocky road of life?

A: When times get tough, I pray for God's direction and comfort. Usually *chocolate* comes to mind, as if the Lord is reminding me that chocolate is comforting and God-given goodness. So I go on the hunt for some chocolate, while God deals with my tough-time issues. We usually get back together to figure out what to do next, but I'm in a better mood to deal with the issues after having some chocolate!

—TAMI COLLINS, PARADISE, CALIFORNIA

haunting quality, as if a timeless story is hidden in the silky layers of sound. As she sang the following words to me, it was easy to picture the little girl she used to be:

Sometimes I feel like a motherless child,
a long ways from home.[2]

Sometimes Children Know Best

You want a sweeter journey in life? Ask yourself a couple of questions:

- *How can I be inspired by my inner child?* Singing, keeping a diary, playing practical jokes, and quacking like a duck might be a good start, but it's *only* a start. Make your own list. What makes *you* feel young at heart?

- *What activities inspired by my actual childhood can help me cope or thrive today?* When I consider the things I loved as a child, I can see the seeds of many of the things I love today. For example, as a kid it was virtually impossible for me to take on any task or project without rallying friends to join me. Maybe because I tend to think life is a grand adventure I don't see the point in traveling alone. Whatever the reason, whether I was producing backyard plays, starting neighborhood newspapers, or building a clubhouse, I always talked my sisters and friends into playing the role of accomplices and partners.

  Similarly, when I think about the things that comforted me when I was little—journaling, long hugs, talking things out, building a fire and spending contemplative hours mesmerized by the dancing flames—well, these same things have the power to comfort me today.

What about you? Are there things that made your life a little sweeter when you were a kid that could do the same for you now that you're all grown up? Don't downplay those things. Kids may be small, but there are a lot of things they do better than adults. For example, kids are unbelievably resourceful. How many grownups can produce a three-act play with nothing more than bed sheets, a card table, and a handwritten script? The next time you feel like you've got a task to do and you're not sure where to start, think like a kid. Look around you and figure out how to turn the everyday resources at your fingertips into the solution you need.

Kids are also masters at exploring life outside the box. In fact, kids don't even realize there *is* a box. They simply think, process, and move forward in fresh ways because, well…because they're kids. Who says *you* have to obey the box? When I was dating K, he told me his grandmother used to say that every morning when she woke up, if she stretched out her hands and didn't feel the sides of a coffin, she knew it was going to be a good day. Whether we're talking about coffins or the confines of limiting paradigms or roles, any day spent outside the box is a good day.

Sweet Secrets

Q: What's your secret to a sweeter journey on the rocky road of life?

A: Sinatra and Tom Jones *real* loud.

—VALERIE DORAN

Kids also aren't afraid to travel without a map. To a kid, even a bad day can be an adventure. Maybe not one you're eager to repeat, but an adventure nonetheless. (If nothing else, it'll leave you with some good stories to tell!) Kids know you can't have *any* adventure (even a bad one!) if you let fear hold you back from lacing up your hiking boots and seeing what's around the bend.

Finally, kids are optimistic. Remember how good life felt before you lost some of the battles that, even today, can make you wince when you think about them? By the time we're all grown up, we've racked up a list of experiences that can sap our confidence in ourselves and our faith in a good outcome. Don't let that happen. Get in touch with your inner child and siphon off some of her optimism. Trust me, she's got plenty to share.

And in the meantime, swing on a swing set. Laugh at ducks. And just in case you're wondering, the best place to store your favorite toy that toots is next to your credit cards and not your cell phone.

Food for Thought

- What can you learn from your inner child? Name one or two things that come to mind.
- What do you do to stay young in spirit or young at heart?
- What have you seen in the lives of others that helps keep them in a joyful or playful mood?
- What is the difference between being childish and childlike?

Because *Real Women* Don't Need a *Cookbook*

Chocolate Kisses

For an immediate, zero-calorie, chocolate quick fix,
try the Cocoa Shoppe's cocoa lip balms. They're
made with real Omanhene chocolate and come in six
flavors! Dark chocolate espresso bean, dark chocolate cocoa noir, milk chocolate orange truffle, milk
chocolate mint leaf, white chocolate chai tea, and
white chocolate raspberry tart. If I can't eat my chocolate, at least I can have the taste and aroma on my
kisser. :) I buy mine at www.thecocoashoppe.com.

   —Kiki Weber, Saukville, Wisconsin

Real Cocoa + Real Milk = Real Comfort

I love hot cocoa. I always keep real cocoa mixed with
sugar on hand so I can add it quickly and easily to
steamed or microwaved milk. The whole process
takes under three minutes, and the real milk mixed
with the real cocoa is very soothing.

   —Kelly McCurley, Larkspur, Colorado

For a New Taste in Life, Look for a New Recipe

Sometimes you need to head back to the drawing board—or cookbook, as the case may be.

One summer my family was evacuated from our home near Denver because a wildfire raged just a few miles away. When the call came to prepare to evacuate, I alerted my two children and we began scouring the house for valuables. Within minutes a pile of things-too-precious-to-leave-behind had been deposited by the front door.

The first thing I noticed was the inflatable plastic shark. I said, "What's this shark doing here? We can't take an inflatable shark."

Kacie, then seven, looked at me as if I had suggested sacrificing her sister to a volcano god. She said, "Mom, I *love* that shark. We *can't* leave him here to die in the fire!"

Not wanting to provide more fodder than I already do for my daughters' sessions with their future therapists, we kept the shark.

Kaitlyn, fifteen, added cheer pompoms and her favorite goose-down pillow.

I grabbed the avocado green KitchenAid mixer that had sat in my mom's kitchen for years. When my grandmother died, her KitchenAid got passed down to my mom, who then gave me her own. Under those circumstances, what woman wouldn't save a mixer?

We rounded up the dogs, fish, photo albums, and Kacie's collection of several thousand Chuck E. Cheese prize tickets (she's saving for the Grand Am). Kaitlyn rescued the Texas license plate she had salvaged from our former car.

Outside, gray ash covered our car and the air smelled bitter and smoky. We loaded down my SUV with our salvaged treasures, and as we were pulling away from the house, Kacie proudly brandished a small plastic bag of gum. She said, "Look, Mom, I saved the Dubble Bubble!"

I said, "Thank God. Now we won't have to turn around."

Back to Life's Cookbook

We spent the next two weeks with family in Colorado Springs. Every day we eyed smoky skies and watched the news. As the wildfire continued to spread, I tried to prepare my daughters for the worst. I said, "Years from now, out of the blue, you'll suddenly remember something that was lost in the fire, something precious you'd forgotten about until that moment. When that happens, take a moment to think about it—close your eyes, take a deep breath—then let it go."

We were lucky. Our house was spared. But the prospect of losing everything in a fire did give me lots to ponder. I couldn't help but think we are not unlike small planets, each one of us our own center of gravity. As we orbit through life, we gather things to us: belongings, relationships, dreams. With these things in hand, we go to great pains to build some sort of personal civilization. But sometimes we lose it all and have to start from scratch.

You've probably never lost everything you own in a wildfire (and thank God, neither have I). But undoubtedly, things have happened that have forced you to regroup and perhaps even reinvent a portion of your life—starting from scratch. If it wasn't a wildfire, perhaps it was bankruptcy. Or divorce. Or the death of a dream or a cherished relationship. Perhaps you lost your home in foreclosure or your job in a recession, or suffered a serious illness that rocked your world.

The fact is that sometimes things happen, and whatever recipes we had been following before no longer apply to our lives. Hard as it is, there are times when we are forced to come up with brand-new plans.

Embracing a New Vision for Life

For Erik Weihenmayer, the thing that forced him to reinvent his life was going blind at the age of thirteen. Erik, who was born with a rare form of retinoschisis, shared his story with me over the phone: "After losing almost all my sight, I didn't know how to reach out, or how to manage my emotions or my future. I was an angry kid with a lot of frustration. I didn't want people to look down on me. I didn't want to receive help without being able to give something in return. I didn't want to sit on the sidelines. It was a tough time."

For a while he tried hanging on to his old dream of being an ordinary kid. Before his sight was completely gone—when he could still see shadows out of one eye—sometimes he'd leave his cane at home, pretending he could see in order to fit in with other kids. One day he and some friends were walking on a dock. He'd left his cane behind, hoping that no one would notice he was blind. But he accidentally stepped off the side of the dock and fell, landing on his back on the edge of a boat.

The accident was a wake-up call. Erik said, "When I look back on that day, I remember thinking, *You're going to kill yourself if you don't make some changes.* At that moment, I realized it didn't matter how much I hated going blind. My feelings were completely irrelevant. I could wish all day long that I could see, or that I was taller, or stronger, or faster. Wishes didn't matter. I told myself, *If you're going to get out of this, you're going to have to be a pragmatist. You're going to have to be brutally honest with yourself. You're going to have to look at what your adversities are in life. Don't sugarcoat them, or look through colored glasses, or try to ignore them. See them for what they are, assess them, then figure out what you need to do to climb out.*"

Sweet Secrets

Q: What's your secret to a sweeter journey on the rocky road of life?

A: Find others who really need something— anything—and do all you can to help them get it: kindness, self-esteem, money, baby-sitting, conversation, food, comfort, God—whatever they need most.

—JOHN KOITER, COLORADO SPRINGS, COLORADO

Erik's new recipe for his life didn't include denial. It didn't include mediocrity. It didn't include excuses. It didn't even include trying to be ordinary. He began pursuing his new plan with a passion. Indeed, the new approach to adversity that Erik adopted the day he fell off a dock changed the direction of his entire life. He became a high school teacher and then a world-class adventurer. In 2001 he became the only blind man in history to reach the summit of the world's highest peak, Mount Everest. He also has completed a seven-year quest to climb the Seven Summits, the highest peaks on each of the seven continents. He's been on the cover of *Time* magazine and is the subject of a variety of documentaries and movies, including *Touch the Top of the World,* an A&E Movie of the Week.

He is also serious about helping other people (with and without disabilities) expand their personal boundaries and live more passionately. In addition to organizing expeditions for teams of blind and sighted teens, Erik has been joined by Mark Wellman (the first paraplegic to climb the three-thousand-foot face of El Capitan) and Hugh Herr (a double-leg amputee and scientist at Harvard's prosthetics laboratory) in launching No Barriers, a nonprofit organization that teaches people with special challenges how to use the most innovative technologies and techniques. Every year the No Barriers Festival brings together hundreds of scientists, inventors, artists, athletes, and outdoor enthusiasts—most of whom have a disability.

The boy who fell off a boat dock because he wanted to pretend he wasn't blind is, today, scaling mountains, assembling teams of disabled and able-bodied adventurers of every age, and helping to test and even create the world's most cutting-edge assistive tools and techniques. Best yet, he is teaching and inspiring others to push past their personal boundaries so they can live extraordinary lives.

Today Erik says, "There's a kind of adversity that you don't ask for, and a kind you ask for because you want to make things happen." He adds, "Adversity is like a two-sided coin. When you come up against adversity, it can feel like a brick wall. It can diminish you. That's the first side of the coin. But when you break through that wall and surprise yourself, that process gives you energy, it redefines your attitude for your entire life. That's the second side of the coin."[1]

And it all began when Erik made the choice to let go of his vision for a life of fitting in and being normal. When he finally let go of ordinary, he was able to grasp with both hands a new vision that was nothing less than extraordinary. (To learn more about Erik's story or to follow his ongoing adventures, go to www.touchthetop.com.)

Letting Go

One night my phone rang at midnight. It was Skippy. That's not his real name, of course. I gave him that nickname in one of my books because I was mad at him. We had fallen in love four years earlier, took turns breaking each other's hearts, and then he moved to another state.

By the time I got that midnight phone call, Skippy had been living on the other side of the country for two years. He had fallen in love with someone else. I'd fallen in love with someone else too. We'd recently started talking again by phone, however, which is how I learned that his relationship with Theresa was over, and how he knew that my relationship with K had come to an end as well.

Skippy and I chatted for a couple of minutes before he blurted, "I'm tired of fighting this. I still love you. You're my soul mate, and I don't care about the stuff that broke us up. I love you and I want to move back to Colorado and marry you."

His words were sweeter than chocolate.

There were a couple of small hitches, however, to getting hitched:

Skippy had gone back to school and was in the middle of a two-year program. So a move to Colorado would mean losing months of work. Could we maintain a long-distance relationship for eighteen months until he graduated? Plus, a lot had happened in both of our lives since we'd been apart. Had too much water flowed under the bridge?

We decided to find out. We talked every day on the phone, got video cameras for our computers, researched airfares, planned trips back and forth, and spoke often about the future. We did our best. But try as we might, we couldn't find a way to rediscover the rhythm that had once been ours. After a while we stopped talking about a future altogether, barely making references to five days from now much less five years. The shift was glaringly obvious. An elephant had not only entered the room, it was sitting on our laps.

Some days I'd say, "We're going to have to talk about it at some point." Skippy would answer, "We will, I'm just not ready yet."

Other days he'd say, "We should talk about it soon, I guess…" I'd say, "I know, but maybe not quite yet."

Eventually we stopped putting it off and had a long heart-to-heart. We agreed that it wasn't working. And after everything we'd been through! All the breakups, all the tears. In the end, we said three little words to each other. They were words we had never said before, words that—after loving each other for more than five years—I'd never thought we'd say.

He said, "I release you."

I said, "I release you too."

In Praise of Plan B…and C…and D…

As I was sitting at my kitchen table typing those words about Skippy, Kacie came downstairs and walked past me carrying a pile of clothes.

I said, "What are you doing?"

"Laundry."

"At five-thirty in the morning? You can't do laundry at five-thirty in the morning. It won't dry, anyway, before you have to leave for school. Plus the washer and dryer are next to Mame's room. It'll wake her up."

"But I don't have anything to wear to school! What am I supposed to do?"

"Go to Plan B," I suggested. "Pick one thing, wash it by hand, and dry it with a hair dryer."

A few minutes later I walked upstairs to see if I could give her a hand. She'd washed her shorts by wearing them in the shower. Now she was drying them with the hair dryer. I said, "Lemme do that and you finish getting ready."

Taking the shorts into my bathroom, I ran the hair dryer on them for ten minutes. They were still wet. I realized at this rate they'd never be dry in time. We needed a Plan C. Thank goodness I thought of one!

Fifteen minutes later Kacie came back downstairs for breakfast. She found me, once again, sitting at the kitchen table. Glancing around the room she said, "I don't see my shorts. Where are they? Are they dry?"

I said, "I'll check," and grabbed the oven mitts.

So Much for "Normal"

Look, I don't know why we don't get to live the normal life we thought we'd live, or marry the guy we thought we would marry, or even get to dry our shorts using traditional means like Maytags instead of a cookie sheet and an oven. But I do know that the ability to adjust, regroup, and embrace a new plan—and a new plan after that and even a new plan after that—is one of the most important secrets for experiencing a sweeter life. And this is true no matter what comes our way.

I admire people who can reinvent themselves and keep on truckin' despite the hairpin curves they encounter on their journeys. Erik Weihenmayer is an inspiring example—scaling mountains and leading others to do impossible things. I admire what Skippy's doing as well—going back to school and preparing for a position in health care, reinventing his career and his life in the process.

Cathy Flandermeyer, manager of a bookstore on the campus of New Life Church in Colorado Springs, told me about a hairpin curve that took place in her life. She and her husband, Bill, had to reinvent their financial lives after medical bills forced them to declare bankruptcy and sell their house. At about the same time, events were taking place in Cathy's life that forced her to reevaluate her emotional well-being and her identity.

"The bankruptcy was like bitter topping on a very bitter cake," she said. "For two years, my mom had been living with us and we'd been

Sweet Secrets

Q: What's your secret to a sweeter journey on the rocky road of life?

A: Watch my favorite comedy movies or shows with my favorite comic actors. Laughter, for me, anyway, heals a lot of wounds.

—DIANNE

her caretakers. Mom had always been very hard on me, but her illness stripped away any refinement, and suddenly her criticism turned brutal. She lived with us for two years and was verbally abusive the entire time. When she started getting physically abusive, we had no choice but to send her somewhere where they could care for her and handle her outbursts as well.

"Shortly after Mom left, we had to sell our house. It was such a dark time. I felt as if I'd been beaten up and abandoned. I realized I'd spent too much of my life trying to be what Mom wanted me to be rather than what God wanted me to be."

Cathy was faced with the challenge of reinventing her life on several levels. One day her husband, who had worked for many years as a consultant to retail bookstores, came home from spending the day with one of his clients. Bill found Cathy in the kitchen and got right to the point.

"How would you like to be a bookstore manager?" he asked.

Cathy, who had just started looking for work after years of being a full-time homemaker, blinked in surprise. "I don't fit the mold, Bill! I'm not a warm, fuzzy people person. I'm an organizer. An administrator. Plus, I've never held a job like that in my life!"

"Would you like to give it a shot?"

She said, "What if I fail?"

He said, "They need you."

Cathy surprised herself by saying, "Okay, sure."

That was five years ago. Today when she talks about her career, she can't help but smile. "I've never loved a job like I love this one. I can't wait for Mondays! Turns out I have a natural talent for this sort of thing. Who knew?"

Cathy is also at peace. "As we started to get past the dark time with my mom and with the bankruptcy, good things started to happen. Bill has a great job, I have a great job, *and* we love the house we're living in.

When we sold our house, we knew we'd miss little things we loved, like having a gas stove and electric oven, the huge mirrors in the master bathroom with medicine cabinets behind every mirror, not to mention the elevation and the views. Well, guess what? The house we're renting has every one of those things. We feel like we're being blessed at every turn, like God has been pouring warm oil all over us. Sometimes, when I pray, I tell him, 'Wow, you never did leave us, did you?'"

Cathy says she's at such peace that she no longer binge-eats for stress relief and comfort. She's lost thirty-five pounds. But more important, she says she's learned not to let the dark seasons define her. She's also at peace with knowing that the rich times—like now—don't define her either.

"The next time we face loss or hardship—and I'm sure we will—I'll be better prepared. I won't be so afraid or have so much doubt. I have a much clearer picture of who I am and who God is. He's so much bigger than we think. He loves us more than we think. Best of all, no matter what we go through—good times or tough times alike—God really does have a plan and he'll make a way for us, even if it's nothing at all like what we expected!"[2]

Life Is Like a Big Dish of Tiramisu

I'm not going to wax philosophical and tell you that Plan B (or C or D or even X, Y, or Z) always turns out better than Plan A. I have no idea if it does or doesn't. But here's what I do know. No matter how many times you and I have to go back and reinvent our lives, as long as we're still kickin', we still have the opportunity to taste and see that life is good. In fact, better than good. Like tiramisu, actually, with all these fabulous rich layers—some sweet and some not-so-sweet—that make up the generous experience of being alive.

Wildfire. Bankruptcy. Divorce. The death of a dream or relationship. Unexpected disability. The loss of home or job. Sometimes things happen that send us scrambling, and we have to begin again. If we're lucky, we get to carry a few treasured ingredients from the season we're leaving into the new lives we're starting to create. But even when we don't, well…we're a hardy lot. We grieve. We survive. In time, we can even thrive again.

With or without the inflatable shark.

Food for Thought

- Is there something or some things you're afraid of losing? If so, what?

- We rarely have to start from scratch in every area of our lives. Even as my daughters and I got ready to evacuate our home, we knew that we still had one another—even if we were to return to a pile of ashes. I still had my job. And my friends. And more than enough Dubble Bubble. Even if you lost the thing(s) you identified in the previous question, what would you still have in your life?

- Have you ever had to reinvent a portion of your life? What helped you do that?

- A newspaper columnist by the name of Mad Dog wrote, "People reinvent themselves for different reasons.... You'd figure reinvention might have to do with lack of success, but that just isn't true." He believes that people should reinvent themselves at least once during their lifetimes.[3] What are your thoughts?

ري What does failure look like to you? Do you consider that having to go to Plan B is a sign of failure, or of tenacity and courage? What about Plan W?

Because *Real Women*
Don't Need a *Cookbook*

Fab Fondue

I have this amazing chocolate fondue dip. First you rub the walls of a small Crock-Pot with a teaspoon of butter. Then drop in eight Hershey's plain chocolate bars and let them melt. Add one to two tablespoons of milk and one cup of miniature marshmallows. Gradually add a half cup of whipping cream and stir. Let the mixture slow cook for about two hours. Then dip in pieces of banana, marshmallows, strawberries, pound cake, or vanilla wafers, and enjoy!

—Chelsea Orist, Colorado Springs, Colorado

Chocolate-Covered Bacon Lollipop, Anyone?

Weird food combinations aside,
sometimes we have to relax and
live with stuff we never thought
would go together.

What do you get when you mix chocolate and bacon? Apparently, you get a taste phenomenon that has been quietly sweeping the nation since 2005. Google the words *chocolate* and *bacon* and see how many results you get. I got almost five million.

Who knew?

There are some combinations that, the minute you hear them, you think, *That'll never work.* I once found a recipe online for vanilla breast-milk cupcakes with strawberry frosting. Okay, who would even come up with that? (And more important, *why?*)

I've always been fascinated by the juxtaposition of unlikely elements. This is why I love reading Dave Barry. What a wordsmith! Notice his meticulous positioning of imagery that is unrelated, perhaps even diametrically opposed, in this well-crafted paragraph:

What could be more fun than an outdoors barbecue? I can think of several things offhand, such as watching the secretary of state fall into a vat of untreated sewage.[1]

The unlikely collage of barbecues, politicians, and cesspools may be strange but, then again, maybe it's not as strange as it first appears. After all, one of the regular challenges we face in life is making peace with seemingly incongruous combinations of events, circumstances, and even emotions. My friend Bradley is dealing with the breakup of a relationship. Today he asked me, "Is it weird that we've been broken up for two months and I'm still in love with her?" One woman I know, newly widowed, juggles grief over her husband's death with joy over the upcoming marriage of her daughter.

I know women whose military husbands are deployed overseas. One woman told me that when her husband is gone, she feels all at the same time as if her life must go on and as if her life is put on hold.

My friend Jaqueline despised her healthy body for its ten extra pounds, yet grew to love and accept her body when it showed the ravages of colon cancer.

Sweet Secrets

Q: What's your secret to a sweeter journey on the rocky road of life?

A: Chocolate! The darker the better. ;-)

—BETH GROUNDWATER

Love and absence.

Grief and joy.

Waiting and not waiting.

Love and imperfection.

Breast milk and cupcakes.

Bacon and chocolate.

Who knew such things were possible?

A Smorgasbord of Human Emotions

When I first read about Erik Weihenmayer, the blind adventurer who scales the tallest mountains in the world, I was fascinated. When I read that he is married, I became fascinated with his wife's story as well. I wrote Ellen Weihenmayer and asked her for an interview. I explained, "I'm guessing that a woman who made the decision to marry and raise a family with a blind adventurer is not a woman who runs screaming from life's challenges. I'm guessing you have wisdom and resources that leave you confident that you'll be able to navigate whatever rocky roads come your way, and I, for one, would love to hear more about that."

Then I asked her to share two or three gems of insight that she's gleaned so far in life. She answered by e-mail, and her answer was nothing like what I'd expected. Instead of focusing on how she coped, she told me her story. And as I finished reading her e-mail, I realized she'd given me more than a few random gems. She'd given me the mother lode. Here is what she wrote:

When I met Erik, he was a schoolteacher. Although he had joined his dad and brothers on mountain treks all over the world, he hadn't climbed any big mountains yet. While we dated, I stayed in the shadow while Erik and his guide dog got all the attention. We shared a love for teaching and the Arizona desert. Erik developed an intense passion for climbing. I helped him when others couldn't go with him. I learned how to set up belay stations and shouted out holds that I thought Erik could reach. On days he was out climbing with friends, I waited until the sun set to hear from him. His phone call was always a welcomed relief.

Soon, I realized that Erik wasn't going to stay with his teaching job for very long. He had other dreams, and the kind of dreaming that he did intrigued me. I had found someone extraordinary! At about that time, he started training to climb Mount McKinley.

On Mount McKinley, as with all mountains he's climbed, I felt like such an insignificant partner. I couldn't train with him; he was so much stronger. The most I could do was ride my bike, with Erik running behind me for miles. We'd attach ski poles to the seat of my bike, and he'd hold on for steering. It was dubbed the blind dragger. His mountain climbing would change the way the world imagines a blind person to be. His mountain climbing, to me, meant that I was going to miss him. I was going to worry. When I saw McKinley the first time, it erupted through the clouds. I was speechless—and nauseated. How could he climb that?!

I was joined by Erik's dad and his brothers in a tiny Cessna plane to witness his last steps up this monster of a mountain. Tears poured down my face as I saw the struggle to the top. The scenery was stunning. We were blessed with good timing; our plane circled overhead while they were summiting.

Still, I came to the realization that climbing is not, at least for me, a spectator sport. It's just too hard to watch a blind man—your husband, the blind man—climb.

When he climbed Everest, I told myself I wasn't going to celebrate the summit. Only his return to base camp. I surprised everyone by screaming and jumping cartwheels upon hearing of his summit. Still, I didn't sleep that night. The climb down is always the toughest.

So, roadblocks. We've been very blessed. I have literally traveled the world, joining Erik on many of his adventures. We got married on Kilimanjaro! Erik is successful. I work for him part-time while orchestrating life with two kids, ages eight and ten. Emma, my older child, is growing up way too fast. Arjun, adopted from Nepal just two years ago, challenges my parenting skills. I manage my life, the kids, the house, the husband, the car, the bills, the shopping, the lawn, the cooking, the cleaning, the doctors' visits, the trash, the shin-guard searches, the violin tuner, the homework, the… You get it. Erik calls me the General.

I think the roadblock is the fact that while I support the dream, I'm not always *in* the dream. To live an extraordinary life, you have to let someone else do the ordinary. Somehow that has become me. I'm working on branching out. I think it's not okay for mothers to just take time to "read a good book." I think we should be doing some of the things we read about. My friend interested me in a surfing/yoga retreat. It was awesome. I started swimming again and placed third in the state two years in a row. Indoor soccer keeps me humble. I want to sleep at night without worry. And in my sleep, I want to dream my own dreams.[2]

Every time I read Ellen's story, I marvel at the banquet of poignant images she has laid out for us. What a smorgasbord of human emotions! Can you hear the pride in her voice as she talks about the extraordinary dreams of the extraordinary man she married? wistfulness as she talks about putting her own dreams on the back burner? Do you sense, as I do, the delicate tension between fear and celebration? between sleepless nights and victory cartwheels? between dreams fulfilled and unfulfilled? between waiting behind and branching forward?

Living with Paradox Is Like Rowing a Boat

What is the definition of *paradox*? *Paradox* is not "contradiction," two mutually exclusive ideas battling it out to see which one will survive and reign. It's not even, as John Koiter suggested with tongue in cheek, a couple of surgeons.

Instead, paradox is the coexistence of two very unlike realities. It's not that one is right and the other is wrong; they may both be true, even though they may *seem* to contradict each other.

Not long ago I read a post on livingparadox.blogspot.com, the blog of a young Muslim woman who journals about her life as an educated woman in Libya. She was a medical student and now is a doctor. She wrote, "I fall and I pick myself up. I lose hope yet I dream. I am lost and I find myself again. I cry and I laugh through my tears. I despair yet I believe."[3]

Paradox is, clearly, the story of our lives.

I received an e-mail from a woman who told me about her life following the death of her daughter. The subject line of her e-mail read, "Maybe not thriving, but definitely surviving." She wrote:

My daughter, Melissa, died on April 1, 2007, from cancer. She was my only child and my best friend. It is a loss from which I will never entirely heal, but I am able to put my feet on the floor each morning and be grateful for the blessing of having been Mom to the coolest human on the planet for nearly seventeen years, because a portion of every day, I devote myself to providing support to other parents whose children are facing critical illness or other medically fragile conditions. My Chicago-area not-for-profit was cofounded by me and my daughter about a month before she died, as a legacy of her life and the kind of person she was. Next week, we are opening our first national chapter located in Wilmington, Delaware, and serving all of Delaware and the greater Philadelphia region. Perhaps my healing comes from helping others through my firsthand knowledge of the depth of this kind of battle and loss.[4]

Patricia Fragen is the founder of Normal Moments (www.normal moments.org). What strikes me the most about her story is the coexistence in her world of loss and gratitude, of longing backward and going forward, of healing self by helping others. How different her life would be—and the lives of other families with critically ill children—if Patricia had decided she had to experience these things in a linear fashion, one after the other, or not at all. What if Patricia had been convinced she had to resolve her great loss before she could be thankful? Or stop looking backward before she could move forward? Or heal herself before she could help others? What would have happened then?

Nothing would have happened, because it's very likely that Patricia would have stayed stuck and unhealed in her loss and the past.

Try rowing a boat with just one oar. A friend notices your circling rowboat and tries to hand you another oar. But you refuse it, telling her you can't embrace the second oar until you're completely through with the first one. See how far you get.

Paradox is like an Oreo cookie. There's that extra sweet spot in the middle. When we can accept paradox in our lives without wasting energy fighting it, we get the chance to experience double benefits. We get, all at the same time, the fruit of grieving and the fruit of gratitude, the fruit of looking backward and the fruit of moving forward, the fruit of healing and the fruit of helping. Being able to pluck all that fruit, however, means staying within reach of the trees on either side of

Sweet Secrets

Q: What's your secret to a sweeter journey on the rocky road of life?

A: I'm such a coffeeholic that, for me, chocolate and coffee go hand in hand. I head to the nearest coffee shop and get a toffee-nut mocha latte, the biggest size they make, then head back home, turn on the fireplace (if it's somewhat cold outside), and knit. I get in my zone and life becomes a little sweeter.

—DEB BUCKINGHAM, COLORADO SPRINGS, COLORADO

us. Living with paradox keeps us from gravitating too far toward the one or the other. Living with paradox keeps us centered.

There is something, however, that can keep you and me from finding that sweet spot in the middle. It's called all-or-nothing thinking. All-or-nothing thinking says, "I must have only apples or no apples at all. Or only persimmons or no persimmons at all. I'm not a fruit salad, after all." But people who allow all-or-nothing thinking to limit their intake of fruit may find themselves with malnourished spirits; with rickets even, or scurvy.

Living with Paradox Is Like Living with God's Puppy

I remember when we got a Boston terrier puppy. Kacie named him Buddy. Buddy was, as you can imagine, a study in contrasts. The bad news was that he was in a constant state of peeing or pooping or chewing or nipping. The good news was that when Buddy wasn't zinging around the house like a loose balloon, he loved to cuddle.

The bad news was that when Buddy cuddled, he also passed gas. (Bostons have short little noses, which means they snort, taking in a lot of air. And that means they emit a lot of air, usually after imbuing that air with lower-gastrointestinal aromas.) The good news was that Buddy was highly entertaining, what with constantly collecting things from around the house and dragging them into his sleeping crate.

I thought this was cute, as long as he was commandeering stuff like Kaitlyn's gym shorts or Kacie's Happy Meal toys. But one morning Buddy and I both spied something of mine lying on the floor. We each dashed for it. I got there first, which was a good thing. Trust me, the last thing I want to see before my first cup of coffee is a four-pound

Boston terrier trotting across the room carrying the plastic case containing my diaphragm.

A couple of weeks after Buddy arrived, Kacie and I were driving somewhere. Suddenly she said, "You know, the first time I laid eyes on Buddy, I fell in love with him and thought he was the perfect puppy. Now he's not so perfect."

I said, "Cool. You've figured it out."

She said, "What?"

I said, "You've figured out 'the secret' that applies to every relationship in the world, including relationships with puppies, best friends, and even husbands and wives. The secret that says when you first meet someone, you think he or she is perfect. But soon you discover that's *not* true! You've figured out the truth, which is that nobody gets a perfect puppy. Or a perfect person either. But we just love one another anyway and get through life the best we can."

Kacie thought a moment and said, "Except God."

I said, "What?"

She answered, "You said no one gets a perfect puppy. Except God. God's puppy would be perfect."

I said, "Okay, sure. If God had a puppy, I'm sure it would be a perfect one."

We drove in silence for a few minutes, and suddenly I began to laugh. I said, "Kacie, I take that back. I don't think God's puppy would be perfect at all. I think it would pee and poop and chew and nip and dart, just like Buddy."

"No way, Mom!"

"And here's how I know that God wouldn't insist on having a perfect puppy: Because he doesn't even insist on having perfect children. His children—that's us—are a mess! We make mistakes all the time. And we get grouchy. And we disobey. And sometimes we're a nuisance, just like Buddy. And you know what? He loves us anyway."

The Bible is filled with paradoxes. Just check out a passage in Matthew 5:3–12 known as the Beatitudes. In this passage, poor folk own the titles to kingdoms and the meek possess the earth. Or how about the verse in Matthew 20:16? "The last will be first, and the first will be last." What does that mean, anyway?

But perhaps the greatest paradox is the love story between a perfect God and imperfect men and women. Somehow, coexisting in this story is a God who is perfectly righteous and cannot wink at any sin or imperfection, and a bunch of humans who are perennial mess-ups. You have a God who hates sin but loves the folks doing the sinnin'. A God who demands separation from imperfection while embracing those of us who are imperfect.

How does this all work?

No one knows, exactly. Paradox and mystery go hand in hand. But I do know that the answer—even if we don't get the mechanics of it—lies in Jesus, who in life and death and resurrected life provided a bridge that allows the meeting of God and humanity, perfection and imperfection, judgment and love.

When I told John I was writing a chapter on living with paradox, he agreed with me that enjoying a sweeter life means knowing how to let go of the need to resolve the many inconsistencies in life. As John put it, "We can spend so much time focusing on trying to stamp out paradox in our lives that we're not truly living."

If your life has elements that appear to be contradictions, relax. Take a deep breath. Now let it out slowly and remind yourself that life is good, even when all the pieces don't fit nicely into carefully labeled boxes. Like Ellen Weihenmayer, be willing to celebrate even when you're afraid. Or like Patricia Fragen, find a way to grieve your loss even as you are grateful for what you had. And like our Libyan friend, allow yourself to dream even when you lose hope, to believe even when you despair, and to laugh through your tears.

What you don't have to do is try the chocolate-covered bacon lollipop. There are some paradoxes that even chocolate can't make up for.

Food for Thought

- Are you an all-or-nothing sort of girl? If so, how has this helped you or hurt you in the past?
- When you're bumping along on a rocky stretch of life, what do you do to appreciate the beauty of your surroundings, even if you wish you were in a better place?
- Even if something is imperfect, can it still have a place of value in your life?
- How do you make peace with the paradoxes in your life?

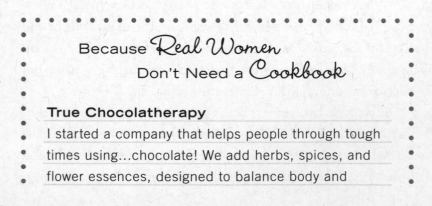

Because *Real Women* Don't Need a *Cookbook*

True Chocolatherapy

I started a company that helps people through tough times using...chocolate! We add herbs, spices, and flower essences, designed to balance body and mind—herbs for adrenal support and essences of flowers for stress reduction. Chocolate is the perfect vehicle for this because of its inherent health benefits (when made right!) and natural, soothing qualities.

When you're looking for the perfect chocolate fix, technique matters! Put the chocolate in your mouth, and let your body heat melt it. Don't get your teeth involved. Let your mind rest in the present moment, totally enjoying the texture and flavor. When you're finished, carry that awareness (and smile) with you throughout your day.

—Lisa Reinhardt, Phoenix, Arizona, CEO Wei of Chocolate (www.weiofchocolate.com)

10

Who's Your Daddy?
(If He's a King, What
Does That Make You?)

 Sometimes it's not what you know
or even who you know. Sometimes
what really matters is how you're
related.

It's been several months since Kacie first developed that crush on Robert Faugno. In case you don't remember Robert from chapter 1, he works at Carlo's Bakery in Hoboken, New Jersey, which is featured on *Cake Boss,* a reality show on the Food Network. Kacie thinks she and Robert should get married one day. Robert has yet to discover that Kacie exists. I'll let you know how it turns out.

In the meantime we're not too worried that Robert hasn't proposed yet. After all, he lives more than sixteen hundred miles away. Plus, he's busy. Being related to the master baker of a world-renowned bakery comes with a lot of responsibility. Apparently it also comes with a few perks, like having a spectacular young woman in Colorado fall madly in crush with you. And all of this simply because his uncle is a famous master baker.

I too know what it's like to enjoy perks based solely on my relationship with someone who is influential. When I was a teenager, my parents owned a printing company. My dad kept a running tab at the corner gas station. On my way home from school or a football game, I often pulled our red Ford Ranchero up to the pumps—they were all full-service back then—and told Jim, the attendant, to "fill 'er up." He did, and all I had to do was sign the charge slip, which added the purchase to my dad's account. Now *that* was a nice perk!

Here's another example. My mom's parents, Demos and Rose Shakarian, owned the world's largest privately owned dairy when I was a teenager. What's more, they were pioneers of the drive-in dairy. Reliance Dairy Farms drive-in stores could be found on street corners throughout Southern California. I remember riding shotgun in my mother's car, with my sisters in the backseat, as Mom pulled into the driveway of the dairy. An attendant would greet us at the car window, ask what we needed, and return a few minutes later with a cardboard box filled with everything we'd ordered. We could get fresh eggs, milk, cheese, and bread, half-and-half for coffee, and maybe even a box of ice cream bars without even leaving the car. Of course, there was never any charge. We were family.

My grandparents were also the founders of Full Gospel Business Men's Fellowship International. With more than two thousand chapters worldwide, the fellowship brings men together at weekly luncheons to share their stories of miracles that God had done in their hearts, their families, and their careers. When I was a teen and young adult, every July the fellowship held its annual convention at the

Anaheim Convention Center. For five nights in a row, the convention center would be packed as thousands came to hear speakers and evangelists such as Oral Roberts and Kathryn Kuhlman.

One Saturday morning in July 1979, I was driving through Anaheim with a young man I had just started dating. (We would later marry, but this was early in our courtship. So early, in fact, that he had yet to meet most of my family.) The fellowship's annual convention

Sweet Secrets

Q: What's your secret to a sweeter journey on the rocky road of life?

A: I call my two closest girlfriends and plan a spa day or a GNO (girls' night out), which usually includes something fun and some food. Our latest adventure was a seafood buffet and playing glow-in-the-dark minigolf at a place called U-Puttz.

On our nights out we can talk and laugh and complain about things going on in our lives. Sometimes, depending on the crisis, I can trust that these beautiful ladies will cry and pray with me and remind me that my heavenly Father is watching over me—that he is the one in control and I don't have to be.

—MICHELLE FREEMAN, NEW BOTHWELL, MANITOBA, CANADA

was underway, and as we passed the Hilton hotel next to the convention center, I knew my family would be staying there. Every year my grandparents were given a beautiful suite as a thank-you for bringing so much business to the hotel. My grandparents were usually given the Presidential Suite, which not only took up the entire top floor but also boasted a killer view of Orange County.

I hadn't told my new beau about the fellowship or the convention or the complimentary luxury suite at the Hilton. As he and I drove past the hotel, I simply said, "Hey! My grandparents are staying there! Let's drop in and say hi."

Years later my husband would talk about how when he and I got into the elevator, I hit the button for the very top floor. When we got off the elevator, I knocked on the only door on that entire floor. My grandmother, still wearing her robe before getting dressed for the evening's meeting, greeted us with hugs and ushered us into a beautiful living room. (At this point, my boyfriend was getting the idea that my grandparents must be influential people indeed.)

We were sitting with my grandparents in the living room, eating dates and nuts from a huge fruit basket, when we heard sirens outside. The sirens started in the distance and grew closer and louder until they seemed to stop in front of the hotel. My grandmother said, "That's probably Pat and Shirley."

Sure enough, twenty minutes later there was a knock at the door and my grandmother went to answer it. There stood Pat and Shirley Boone.

Pat Boone made a name for himself as a singer and actor in the 1950s and early 1960s, selling more than 45 million albums, recording thirty-eight Top 40 hits, and starring in more than a dozen feature films. In the early fifties, one of the artists who opened for Pat was a new-kid-on-the-block named Elvis Presley. By the late fifties, Boone was the second biggest artist on the charts, right behind Elvis and ahead of acts such as Ricky Nelson and the Platters.

In the 1960s Pat and Shirley were on the brink of divorce when they had an encounter with God that changed their lives. Not only was their marriage saved, they were quick to tell anyone they met that a deeper relationship with God had sweetened their lives. Soon they were hosting Bible studies in their home for other celebrities, including Doris Day, Glenn Ford, Zsa Zsa Gabor, and Priscilla Presley.[1]

My grandparents had known Pat and Shirley for years and had invited Pat to sing at that evening's meeting. After the Boones arrived at the airport, they were given a police escort to the hotel. As they walked into the suite, they were hugged warmly by my grandparents— and my grandmother was so comfortable with these longtime friends that she was still wearing her robe!

My boyfriend and I left shortly after that. In the elevator on the way down, he turned to me and asked, "Who *are* you?"

Original or Extra Crispy?

Being related to the right people can get you free gasoline. It can get you free eggs and milk. It can even give you access to places and people to which you might not ordinarily have access. And sometimes, being related to the right people can even help you win a bet.

A few months ago I got a call from Kacie during her school lunch break. As soon as I answered the phone, my fifteen-year-old blurted, "Mom, tell the story about the chicken. I'm putting you on speakerphone."

I guessed, correctly, that she was putting me on speaker for the benefit of her lunch-table friends. So I ran through the story in record time, just in case the class bell was about to ring. Here's the story I told:

When Kacie's grandpa was a little boy, his parents owned a gas station and roadside diner called The Blue Moon Café. There was another restaurant across the street owned by a man named Harland Sanders. Mr. Sanders sold hot dogs and hamburgers. His restaurant did okay, but business could have been better.

One day Kacie's great-great-aunt Cora got a job cooking at Mr. Sanders's restaurant. She was already known around town for her great cooking. In fact, at every church picnic, people practically stood in line to get a piece of Aunt Cora's fried chicken, which she made from her very own recipe using eleven herbs and spices.

When she went to work for Harland Sanders, she started making her special chicken for his restaurant. Pretty soon, there were lines out Harland's door every Sunday afternoon as people showed up to get a plate of Aunt Cora's famous chicken. And, of course, we all know what happened then. But what few people know is that the famous KFC recipe is none other than the recipe of our very own Aunt Cora!

Kacie said gleefully, "Thanks, Mom! Love you! Bye!" and hung up. Later I found out some boy had bet fifty bucks that Kacie's claim about Aunt Cora wasn't true. I said, "Fifty bucks!"

Kacie laughed. "I let him off the hook. Just seeing his face when you told everyone it really was Aunt Cora's recipe was payment enough!"

The truth is, I shouldn't have been surprised to get this kind of phone call from Kacie. She's been asking me to tell people about our connection to KFC ever since she was a kid. Once, when she was about five, we were having lunch with some out-of-town friends. Kacie turned to me all excited and said, "Mom! Tell them the story about Kentucky Fried Chicken!"

One of the women turned to Kacie and said, "Oh, how nice! Are you related to Colonel Sanders?"

Kacie beamed and said, "No! We're related to the chicken!"

Apparently, whether the relative in question is person or poultry, the perks of relationship can be worth crowing about.

"I Want to Be a Princess"

A few weeks ago I had the privilege of speaking to a wonderful group of women at a weekend retreat. I was scheduled to speak four times, and after my second session I was approached by a beautiful young woman. After Sara introduced herself, she said, "I'd like to talk to you about something, but I'd like to think about it a little bit more first." We made arrangements to talk after the evening session.

We got our chance around nine that night, sitting down at an

Sweet Secrets

Q: What's your secret to a sweeter journey on the rocky road of life?

A: Pray a lot and then reach out to a friend to experience God's love with skin on it! A good friend will share her light when yours has gone out. A really good friend will give you a quick shot of motivation or a loving kick in the pants.

—SHARON RAMSEY HANSEN, VIA FACEBOOK

empty banquet table in the meeting room. Sara said, "It's about my self-esteem. I have cerebral palsy, and I feel worthless, like trash." Tears welled up in her eyes as she poured out her story. She talked about the hardships of her life, including her disease, being raped as an adolescent, struggling to lose weight, and recently, losing hard-won independence when she got laid off from her job and had to move back in with her family.

I said, "Sara, what would you like me to pray with you about?" On one hand, it seemed like a silly question; her story had revealed so many needs! But I still wanted to know, specifically, what was heaviest on her heart.

She didn't hesitate for a moment. She said with conviction, "I want to feel like a princess!"

We prayed. One of the things I asked God to do for Sara is, every time she looks in the mirror, for her to see herself the way God sees her and not as other people see her.

After we prayed, Sara said she wanted to buy one of my books. We walked to the book table at the back of the room. She picked out one book, and I gave her two more as a gift. When she pulled out her money for the first book, I told her it was a gift as well. She shook her head and smiled so broadly she actually glowed. "I want to pay for that one. My brother gave me some money and told me to buy myself something at the retreat, and I want to buy your book."

I took the money.

Then, as she was leaving, I put one more book on her pile. "It's a children's book," I told her, "but I think you might enjoy it."

The next morning as the meeting reconvened, Sara found me and gave me a very long hug. She was beaming so much she was practically iridescent.

Holding my two hands in hers, she said, "I couldn't sleep last night, and I didn't want to wake up my roommates, so I went in the bathroom and turned on the light so I could talk to God. And as I was praying, it was as if I heard God say to me, *Sara, I think about you every day.*"

Sara, I think about you every day. What a beautiful message! At her words, I got goose bumps. I'm getting them again, even now, as I write this part of the story.

She continued, "And then I started reading your books. I started with the children's book, and I couldn't believe it! The story was about a little princess who didn't think she was a princess because she didn't look or act like one. But her father is the king so that makes her a *real* princess! Then I realized that my heavenly Father is a King so that means I'm a real princess too!"

Several days after I got home, Sara followed up on my invitation to find me on Facebook. We exchanged posts and she wrote, "I feel like a brand-new person on the inside. My spirits have been lifted, and I see myself in a new way."

I don't know what the future holds for this beautiful woman as she continues discovering who she is and what she's worth. But I really do think she's going to be all right. After all, Sara has already embraced a truth that many of us would do well to embrace: that life is sweeter because we are related to a King who not only answers our prayers but also thinks about each one of us every day.

Our All-Powerful Father

"Do you believe in ghosts?" As Rachel asked the question, her eyes grew big and round. Rachel is fourteen and the daughter of a friend of mine. They had dropped by my house for a visit.

Rachel explained that she was worried about her room at home.

Ever since bringing home a Ouija board, she'd felt uneasy when she was in her bedroom. Sometimes her bed shook while she was trying to sleep. She'd since gotten rid of the game, but she couldn't seem to shake the feeling that her room was haunted.

"I don't know about ghosts," I said, "but I do believe there are spiritual beings in the world with us. Some are good and some aren't. I have no idea if spirits are causing the things you feel in your room, but here's what I do know: There is a God who is greater than any other spirits out there. And when we belong to him—when we are adopted into his family through Jesus Christ and God becomes our heavenly Father—we don't have to be afraid of evil spirits or ghosts. And if we feel pestered by ghosts or spirits, we can tell them to go away and leave us alone. We have that authority, because of who our heavenly Father is."

The idea of children operating in the authority of their parents isn't strange at all. It's like going to your dad's workplace and having a clerk tell you, "I'm sorry, customers aren't allowed behind the counter," and you say, "I'm not a customer. My dad works here," and the clerk replies, "Oh! Well, that's different! Go on back!"

The authority we have when we're related to someone powerful can be life changing. Just think of all the perks you receive, for free, when you become God's daughter. For starters, you are adopted into God's family (see Ephesians 1:5). But that is just the start. You're not a slave to fear anymore. Instead, you are a daughter of God and get to call him *Abba*, which means "Daddy" (see Romans 8:14–16).

What's more, being the daughter of God means that

- you are God's own child (see John 1:12).
- you belong to God (see 1 Corinthians 6:19).
- you are chosen (see Ephesians 1:4).

- your heavenly Father lavishes on you the riches of his grace and forgiveness (see Ephesians 1:7–8).
- you have an inheritance (see Ephesians 1:11, NLT) that is guaranteed by God's own Spirit (see Ephesians 1:14, NLT).
- things that happen in your life have a purpose, and everything will eventually work out (see Romans 8:28).
- you have a home in heaven (see Philippians 3:20).
- you don't have to be afraid anymore; instead, through your Father you have access to power and love and self-discipline (see 2 Timothy 1:7).
- you have access, through Jesus, to every kind of spiritual blessing (see Ephesians 1:3).
- when your heavenly Father looks at you, he sees you as holy and blameless (see Ephesians 1:4).
- you can have peace (see Ephesians 2:14).
- you have access to the Father (see Ephesians 2:18).
- you are secure (see Ephesians 2:20).
- you can approach God with freedom and confidence (see Ephesians 3:12).
- you can have a new attitude and lifestyle (see Ephesians 4:21–32).
- you have eternal life (see John 6:47, NLT).
- your heart and mind are protected by God's peace (see Philippians 4:7).
- you are free (see Romans 8:2).
- you are safe (see 1 John 5:18).

Rachel listened as I told her a little about what it means to belong to God. Then I asked, "Do you want to pray right now and tell God you're ready to belong to him?" She said yes right away, so we prayed together. Immediately she became a daughter of the all-powerful Father.

Are You Ready to Be a Princess?

The Bible tells the story of a man—a prison guard, in fact—who asked, "What must I do to be saved?" (Acts 16:30).

Saved from what? You name it. Sin. Shame. Isolation. Being a spiritual orphan. Sara wanted to be saved from feeling worthless. Rachel wanted to be saved from feeling afraid.

What do you need to do to be saved from whatever it is that you long to be saved from? The answer is the same for the prison guard, for Sara, for Rachel, and for you: "Believe in the Lord Jesus, and you will be saved" (Acts 16:31).

Are you ready to feel like a princess? Are you ready to enjoy intimacy, blessings, and even authority through a newfound Father-daughter relationship with the King of the universe? Are you ready for a sweeter life than the one you've been experiencing? A poet and songwriter in the Bible wrote these words: "Taste and see that the LORD is good" (Psalm 34:8).

Take a leap of faith. You have nothing to lose and everything to gain.

Food for Thought

- ✍ Do you believe in God? If so, what do you believe about him? Would you say you are acquainted with God or have a daily, ongoing relationship with him?
- ✍ How would your life be different if you were, indeed, the daughter of an earthly king (or even a president)? What benefits, blessings, or authority might you have that you don't have now?

ﺺ Pat and Shirley Boone have said that discovering a relationship with God through Jesus Christ
helped save their marriage. Reread the list of
benefits that are ours when we belong to God.
Looking at that list, do you see anything that
could help two people have a stronger marriage?
If so, how?

ﺺ If you already have a relationship with God
through Christ, are you fully enjoying all the privi-
leges and responsibilities that God has for you as
a daughter of the King? Or are you still living like
a spiritual orphan?

ﺺ If you don't already have a relationship with God
through Jesus Christ, would you like to? If so,
here's the prayer that Rachel prayed when she
decided she wanted to belong to God. Find a
quiet place and pray this simple prayer: *Jesus,
I trust that through your death and resurrection
you provided the way for me to become a child of
God. I accept all that you've done to give this in-
credible gift to me. I not only believe in you, but
I also have faith in your ability to save me from
everything—including sin, shame, fear, isolation,
and issues of worth—that has been a part of my
life apart from you. Now I'm not apart from you
anymore. I'm a princess. I belong to you, now
and for eternity. Now begin to show me, every
day, what it means to be in an intimate relationship with you. In Jesus' name, amen.*

Because *Real Women*
Don't Need a *Cookbook*

Chocolate Cherry Cake (with Homemade Chocolate Fudge Frosting)

Here is Lori's go-to recipe whenever she or her family needs a chocolate fix!

1 dark chocolate cake mix (I like Betty
    Crocker's Triple Chocolate Fudge)
1 20-oz. can of cherry pie filling (I like
    Comstock Lite Cherry Pie Filling)
1 single serving of unsweetened applesauce
    (the kind you buy for your kids' lunches)
2 eggs

Mix all ingredients by hand until well blended. Bake in greased and floured Bundt pan at 350 degrees for fifty to sixty minutes. Let cool for ten minutes. Run a knife around the cake to loosen from pan. Place a plate over the top and flip over until you hear the *thump* sound. Set aside to cool.

Fudge Frosting

1 c. sugar
5 tbs. (real) butter
1/3 c. milk

1 c. semisweet chocolate (or milk chocolate,
or dark chocolate)

Bring the first three ingredients to a boil in a medium-sized pot. Keep stirring for two minutes, turn off the heat, and stir in the chocolate. Stir mixture until smooth. Pour this luscious fudge sauce over the cooling chocolate cherry cake. Make a double batch of fudge sauce and save it for topping ice cream!

I've even made this in a cupcake pan with cheesecake in the center. I call it My Chocolate-Cherry-Cheesecake Ding-Dongs... Mmm!

—Lori, Alta Loma, California

11

Traveling Rocky Roads?
Don't Leave Home Without
These Four Things

Anyone can benefit from Becky's
road-tested solutions to heartbreak,
disappointment, loss, and hurt.

After being Facebook friends for nearly a year, Becky and I decided
to take our virtual relationship to the next level: lunch at Sienna's in
Castle Rock, Colorado. This was not just any lunch. It included not
only the most amazing spinach and goat-cheese salad I've ever eaten
but also melt-in-your-mouth tiramisu for dessert.

I should mention here that I had met Becky—who is also a
writer—once before, but she doesn't remember the encounter. Thank
goodness for that!

It was about fifteen years ago, when our paths crossed at a publishing convention. Becky gave me an autographed copy of her new-
est book, which, unfortunately, I managed to misplace within ten

minutes. For years I've hoped she didn't find the book shortly after I lost it and think I'd been careless with her gift.

I shouldn't have worried. Turns out Becky and I are a lot alike. For example, when we met for lunch, I got there twenty minutes late. She waved off my apology, saying, "I just got here myself. I would have been stressed about it, but it crossed my mind that you might be late too."

"Really?"

"You and I both write humor. I figured there's a good chance we both have ADD, in which case we'd probably be late together."

I realized at that moment, even if Becky had found the book of hers that I lost fifteen years ago (it turns out she hadn't), a kindred spirit like her wouldn't hold it against me. Besides, after lunch I gave her one of my books, which she accidentally dropped in the sink in the ladies' room, triggering the water sensor on the automatic faucet.

If that doesn't even the score, nothing will.

Lunch and Sisterhood

Our lunch was well seasoned with laughter. But there were serious revelations as well, especially when Becky told me about a tough season she had gone through the year before.

One of Becky's sons, Zane, works out of Seattle for an Alaskan fishing rig, meaning he's often gone from home for up to four months at a stretch. During Zane's absences, his wife, Bella, and their son, Dusty, would stay for long periods with Becky and her husband. (Before Zane and Bella moved their family to the Pacific Northwest when Dusty was three, they lived near Becky and her husband in Denver—and often with them.)

Becky was with Bella when she went into labor with Dusty, and as she made the hard decision to have a C-section. Zane handed newborn Dusty to Becky to hold and soothe while Zane returned to Bella's side. As soon as Dusty's black eyes met Becky's, she was a goner. The new family came "home" to stay with Becky and her husband, where Becky (now Nonny to Dusty) lovingly tended to Bella. Distanced from her stepmother (Bella's mom died when she was three), Bella and Becky grew especially close. In fact, Becky thought of Bella as a daughter rather than a daughter-in-law.

Sadly, after their move to Seattle, word came that Zane and Bella were divorcing. Though Becky and Bella kept in touch and continued to talk openly, divorce has a way of pushing families to choose sides. There was a bad week of miscommunication, and Bella felt too much empathy was going to Zane. She cut off all communication with his family.

Becky felt as if her heart had been ripped out of her body. She told me, "Imagine loving a daughter-in-law so much she's like your own daughter, and loving a grandbaby so much he's like your very own child, and then having a steel door slam down so hard between them and you that you're not sure you'll ever see either one of them again. I was so devastated I could hardly get out of bed."

She remembers that on bad days she'd spend the day crying. On better days she looked for solace from a formula she'd come up with years earlier, during other trials. She explained, "My survival tools have always been prayer, friends, laughter, and tears. I went back to that formula."

Prayer. Friends. Laughter. Tears. What a recipe for healing! Throw in some chocolate and there's a good chance you could fix the world.

I promise that before this chapter is over, I'll tell you what happened in Becky's family. But first, let's take a look at the four elements in Becky's survival formula, starting with tears.

A Little Cry'll Do You Good

What makes crying so cathartic? Henry Maudsley is credited with saying, "The sorrow which has no vent in tears may make other organs weep."[1] Maudsley was an English psychiatrist in the Victorian era, but researchers today are proving him right.

Crying when we're sad makes us healthier by removing toxins from our bodies. Turns out that while happy tears are made up of just tears, sad tears contain toxins that the body generates as a result of sadness or stress. In fact, the toxins that leave your body during a good cry are the same ones that show up in a number of serious diseases.

According to University of Minnesota researchers, who study the chemical composition of tears, crying when we're sad may also lift our moods. This is because sad tears also contain a chemical called leucine-enkephalin, believed to be an endorphin, one of the natural painkillers our brains produce in response to pain or stress.[2] Crying when we're upset also generates adrenalin, which increases blood flow to the skin (this is why we get red, swollen eyelids after crying when we're upset, but not when we cry at the movies). Adrenalin is part of our fight-or-flight system: it gives us a burst of energy and drive to survive.

In addition to removing toxins, producing feel-better endorphins, and energizing us with adrenalin, a good cry may also help us keep our girlish figures. You already knew that bottling up frustration, anger, or sadness is a recipe for health problems, but did you know it can also make you fat? When you and I hang on to stressful emotions, our bodies make more cortisol, another fight-or-flight hormone designed to get us ready for emergencies. Part of the way our bodies prepare for crisis is to slow down our metabolism, increase our cravings for fatty, salty, and sugary carbs, *and* store extra fat! Crying helps us release all of those bottled-up, stressful emotions (reducing the need for all that excess cortisol).[3]

Indeed, it has been said—and rightfully so—that tears are the safety valve of the heart when it's under too much pressure.

Finally, a good cry is a fight for life, one that jars us from the stupor of our pain and awakens us to the task of living again. When I'm filled with despair and feel like giving up, sobbing mandates a burst of energy that defies the lethargy of my despair. Inconsolable crying immerses me in a salty sea of emotions where I wrestle with my frustrations, hurts, and fears. It's an exhausting battle in which nothing is held back, no holds are barred.

Eventually the last sob is spent, and what began as a war cry ends with a ragged sigh. I'm exhausted. I'm also soggy, with runny nose and

Sweet Secrets

Q: What's your secret to a sweeter journey on the rocky road of life?

A: During tough times I have found that my greatest source of encouragement comes from going straight to God in worship and in his Word. After that, I never hesitate to call a friend! I just sent an e-mail, in fact, to a friend with the subject line "Some things are just more fun with you...like lunch!"

—AMY

red-rimmed eyes. But the despair is quiet. If not gone, it's at least as worn out as I am—and I feel better. Perhaps I'm simply too tired to entertain any more thoughts of despair. Or maybe I'm just feeling the afterglow of all the adrenalin and endorphins that accompanied my wild sobbing.

But I think it's more than that. Facing our darkest emotions is like a brush with death. Tempted to slide into quiet hopelessness, we rise up instead. Sometimes, in an extravagant expenditure of passionate tears, we rediscover the strength to go on.

Exercise Your Funny Bone

Another ingredient in Becky's recipe for coping and healing is laughter. How much healing power is there in laughter? We know that a good belly laugh has the power to make us feel better. Laughing makes us healthier in body, mind, and spirit. In fact, it's kind of like jogging for our insides. Laughing burns calories, releases endorphins, and alters brain-wave patterns. It reduces stress, lifts our spirits, and boosts our immune systems![4] Best of all, it has no calories and can't make you pregnant, so there's no reason laughter shouldn't be a first-line defense against the stresses of each day.

It doesn't matter if you're laughing because you think something's funny or because, well…you're forcing yourself to laugh. Really, just start laughing. For no reason. And don't stop. Keep it up for one minute. By the end of that minute, you'll be laughing for real. As in totally cracking yourself up and loving every minute of it! Try it. You're gonna thank me.

Unless, of course, you try this in public. Then you'll be writing me a letter from a padded cell. But even if you end up having to talk yourself out of a psych ward, at least you can do it knowing you have a healthier immune system and have even burned calories. And if that doesn't put a grin on your face, nothing will.

Tears, Laughter, and Prayer

There is a ton of research that says prayer makes a measurable difference in the health and well-being of people who pray. For example, people who pray tend to have lower blood pressure, less depression, lower suicide rates, and stronger immune systems![5]

And get this: science has proven that prayer also makes a difference in the health and well-being of the folks being *prayed for.* In fact, studies prove that sick people who are prayed for by others—even if they don't know they're being prayed for—get better at a faster rate than sick people who don't have others praying for them.[6]

I spoke with Betsey Newenhuyse and Jane Johnson Struck about how the prayers of others help us cope and heal. Betsey is editorial director at Moody Publishers, and Jane is former editor of *Today's Christian Woman* magazine. Together they write *Betsey:Jane,* a blog for women in which they share thoughts on matters of the heart, the home, and our world. (Check it out at http://betseynjanes.blogspot.com.)

Betsey said, "There have been times when I'm struggling and I feel too stressed or distracted to pray. If I know that others are praying on my behalf, it's an inexplicable comfort. It's powerful."

Jane agrees. Fourteen years ago she and her husband, Richard, faced a serious health crisis in their family. She described it as a very tumultuous, scary time. "When people told us they were praying for us, it was like water in the desert," she said, adding that the experience reshaped her perspective on the power of intercessory prayer.

"It's such a precious transaction; you don't want to treat it casually like 'Let's do lunch.' You don't want to tell someone you'll pray for them and not follow through. After our crisis, I realize more than ever that when someone is going through a tough time and you say, 'I'll be praying for you...,' they really count on that."[7]

For novelist Brandilyn Collins, the prayers of people she knew—as well as those of strangers—ushered in a dramatic healing that changed her life. A year after her diagnosis with Lyme disease, Brandilyn was in chronic pain. She wrote, "The disease had attacked my joints like rheumatoid arthritis, my muscles like multiple sclerosis, and my brain's processing like Parkinson's." She needed a cane to walk; her knees were inflamed, and if she had to come down a flight of stairs, she did so sideways and in great pain. Furthermore, this author of more than twenty-one mystery novels could barely read; her brain couldn't process words on a page.

While on a trip to their vacation home in Coeur d'Alene, Idaho, Brandilyn and her husband, Mark, decided to visit a Christian ministry called the Healing Rooms in nearby Spokane. Brandilyn shared, "We'd known about the Healing Rooms for some time... Suddenly I really felt a real urgency to go." They made plans to drive to Spokane on Saturday, May 10.

A few days later Brandilyn received an e-mail from a fellow member of the American Christian Fiction Writers (ACFW), an organization that provides resources and an online community for authors and readers of Christian fiction. Without knowing anything about Brandilyn's upcoming visit to the Healing Rooms, this friend had felt strongly that Saturday, May 10, was to be a day of prayer for Brandilyn. The friend was contacting ACFW members by e-mail, asking them to participate in a twenty-four-hour prayer chain. As complete strangers signed up for fifteen-minute segments around the clock, Brandilyn was amazed. She was more convinced than ever before that May 10 was going to be a turning point.

She said, "Saturday morning I was really hurting, paying for trying to do too much on Friday. I hobbled into the Healing Rooms
using my cane as much as I could, but with a weak upper body, you
can't lean much on a cane." During her visit, two different prayer
teams prayed for her. When they were done, Brandilyn hobbled back
to her SUV. It was difficult for her not to show her deep disappointment. She had hoped the prayers would make a difference. Still, she
decided to praise God for making her well—despite the fact that she
seemed to be in as much pain as ever.

The family began the drive back to Coeur d'Alene. Half an hour
into the trip, Mark stopped so they could get lunch. As Brandilyn
started to climb down from their SUV, it dawned on her that she
didn't need her cane. She was able to walk from the vehicle to the restaurant without help—something she hadn't done in months!

By the time they arrived home, Brandilyn was feeling even better.
She told me, "The pain was gone. My knees were stronger. My elbows
and neck didn't hurt. I felt energy like I haven't felt before. I went upstairs to our bedroom—and walked up the stairs *normally*! Then I
came down them (really hard for weak legs) totally normally.... I let
out a whoop and called the family to come see. So of course I had to
go back up the stairs and come down them again. Normally!"

Brandilyn went straight for her jogging shoes. It seemed crazy—
she hadn't had a reason to wear them in nearly a year—but she couldn't
help herself. She walked a loop around her neighborhood, a third of a
mile, up and down hills she could never have managed the day before,
even with her cane! She walked that loop five times...and during the
last lap, she actually broke into an easy jog!

After her walk—I mean, jog!—Brandilyn checked her e-mail and
found message after message from ACFW members who were praying
for her, still unaware that a miracle was already underway. Many wrote

that as they prayed for Brandilyn, they were surprised at how strongly they felt God's presence.

Brandilyn felt that she couldn't, quite yet, announce what was happening since people would still be praying for her until 10 p.m. her time. "God was continuing to pour out his blessings on ACFW, and that should continue until the end of the prayer time—for the

Sweet Secrets

Q: What's your secret to a sweeter journey on the rocky road of life?

A: How do I make life sweeter in the middle of a crisis? A spa day with some good girlfriends. That could be just going to get nails done—something to distract me for an hour or two. Coffee, chocolate, a good movie, and a good cry will do it too. Lately, I find myself learning how to pray again. Learning to trust the Lord to take my burden when I just can't handle it anymore. I picture myself in my Father's arms, just crying and letting it all out, and all he does is let me cry. He smiles and gives me the security that he is there. Nothing is too big!

—MICHELLE FREEMAN, NEW BOTHWELL, MANITOBA, CANADA

pray-ers and for me. I felt the continued prayers would help my knees right up to the end of the day, and people would continue to be blessed."

By the end of the night, Brandilyn was completely pain free. She got her last e-mail from the woman who had signed up to pray from 11:45 p.m. until midnight. This woman reported, "The song 'Praise Him, praise Him, all ye little children' kept running through my head and interrupting my prayers, so I finally decided to just sing the song and changed my prayer of supplication to a prayer of praise for what I knew God had accomplished that day."

More than seven years later, Brandilyn remains healthy. She jogs every day and maintains an educational blog and online support community for people suffering from Lyme disease. In addition, she has just published her twenty-second suspense novel—*Over the Edge*—about a woman who discovers someone has intentionally infected her with Lyme disease as she is caught up in controversy swirling around it.

Brandilyn also has a newfound passion for praying for people who are going through tough times. About her own debilitating illness and healing she said, "It was a bitter season in my life, but I wouldn't go back and change a thing. I wouldn't be the person I am today without going through what I did. Extracted from that bitter season are so many things that add richness and sweetness to my life today."[8]

Sisterhood Rocks!

Of all the ingredients in Becky's formula, I saved friends until last, and here's why: each of the previous ingredients—tears, laughter, and prayer—is simply sweeter when shared with a friend.

When I think of my own tears, laughter, and prayers over the past year, the presence of family and friends has made all the difference in my world. Indeed, people who love me must have been paying attention when the Bible gave this healing advice: "Laugh with your happy friends when they're happy; share tears when they're down" (Romans 12:15, MSG).

In chapter 8 we met Cathy Flandermeyer, who manages the bookstore at New Life Church in Colorado Springs, Colorado. She said one of the more precious aspects of her job is getting to interact with some of the women who come in to look for books. She said, "Sometimes, before or after one of the church services, I'll see a woman in the bookstore and it's obvious she's really hurting. She'll look like she has the weight of the world on her shoulders. Sometimes she'll have tears in her eyes. I'll go up and say, 'Can I pray with you?' and she'll begin to cry and tell me her story, and then we pray. Sometimes the stories are heartbreaking. But we pray together and cry together, and sometimes it's a balm."[9]

I like the word *balm*. Like Chap Stick on cracked, dry lips, balm is soothing and healing all at once. When we share tears, prayers, and even laughter with a friend—even a friend we've just met!—it can be just that. So where do we go to find good friends like these?

New Girl in Town

Betsey and Jane had known each other for years, through, as Betsey calls it, their shared pedigree in publishing. But it wasn't until Betsey and her husband, Fritz, moved into Jane's neighborhood that the two women decided to take their friendship to a new level.

Betsey wrote, "Not long after we moved, our daughter got married. So what was next for me and Fritz? I'd been thinking about this anyway, about the broad contours of my life, about what was really important. One of the reasons we 'upsized' when we moved was to have a larger home for hospitality (and, Lord willing, grand-children!). I realized that friendship, both with other couples and with women, really mattered to me, and now was the season for cultivation."

Discovering they lived five miles apart gave Betsey and Jane a chance to cultivate something new. Plus, Betsey had been praying for Jane. She said, "Jane had recently retired as editor of *Today's Christian Woman* magazine, and I remember when I'd heard the news, I prayed for her. I knew that leaving a position you've loved for twenty years leaves a void. I knew she would need friends."

Jane wrote, "After I retired…I wondered if I'd ever write again. I felt stale, dried up, overwhelmed by a tough season of elder-care issues [my husband] and I went through last year…. Bimonthly breakfasts with Betsey became that bright spot on my calendar. I knew I could vent about the nuts and bolts of life—the challenges of parenting adult…children, caring for aging parents, dealing with my own aging, loving my husband well, even finding adventure and joy in midlife— and Betsey would understand…. I found myself feeling 'creative' again, much to my delight!"

Today the friends continue to reach out to other women through their blog, and also through a book club they launched with several other women. As Jane said, you can be someone who simply lunches with friends, or you can cultivate the riches from friendships that dig beneath the surface. By digging deeper, you find the friends who "in-quire and encourage and inspire," who help you "feel Not So Alone on this wild ride called life."[10]

Like-minded Folk

Just in case your future best friend doesn't start praying for you, decide to upsize her house, and then move into your neighborhood, another great place to make friends is to seek out gatherings of like-minded folk. Ane Mulligan has written five novels and shared with me over the phone that the journey on which she has felt most alone and lost has been her journey to become a writer. She told me that after years of working hard and developing a thick skin—and "learning to throw out all the words I'd written because they didn't serve the story"—she finally had an editor tell her she was ready to be published.

"That was three years ago," she sighed, "and it hasn't happened yet."

Ane, who has an agent but has yet to receive a publishing contract, added, "I feel called to write. Is God saying, 'I called you here, even if you are never published'? I don't know. All I know is that I can't stop writing. The stories keep coming. Perhaps writers have to come to a place—not where they give up writing, but where they give up publishing. Maybe this is where the magic happens."

For Ane, the sweet secret that keeps her going is the feedback, support, and camaraderie of like-minded folk at ACFW—the same group that coordinated the prayer chain for Brandilyn. "A writer can't do it alone," Ane said. "You have to have feedback, and your mother can't do it, because she adores you. Other writers help you grow and stand with you when those rejection letters come—and they will."

Ane began attending writers' conferences where she met friends and mentors. Eventually she joined a critique group, and several years ago she helped form Pen Writes, a support and critique group with about thirty members. Today, she is an editor with the literary blog

Novel Journey and a humor columnist for ACFW's e-zine, *Afictionado*. She also serves on ACFW's board and has helped launch many of the organization's twenty-three chapters.

She says the conferences and chapters are invaluable for writers longing to feel a part of a larger community. "Otherwise," she quipped, "writing is a lonely profession. You sit alone at your desk with a lot of imaginary friends."[11]

Friend Me

Imaginary friends may not be very talkative, but virtual friends are another matter altogether. In fact, my friendship with Becky started out on Facebook. And even our lunch together came about as a result of a virtual connection. I like what she has done with this social networking tool.

"I was surprised how much comfort there was in this Facebook thing," Becky told me. "When I was heartbroken over losing contact with Bella and Dusty, I could go online and say, 'I'm having a hard time,' and immediately people would respond. Some of these people I know personally; others I don't. Some people told me their own stories of losing contact with a child or grandchild and how eventually everything worked out all right. Other people told me they were praying for me. When you're in a dark place, even prayers from strangers make a difference."

I like how Becky sought comfort from her community. She didn't sit back and wait for people to reach out to her; she reached out first. And people generously poured out hope and prayers in return. And you'll be glad to know that after a very rough four months, Becky's relationships with Bella and Dusty were not only restored but also healed and taken to a newer, closer level. She sees them every few months, and all is right with the world again. In fact, at this writing, a greater miracle is taking place as Zane and Bella have reconciled, and they all are happier than they've ever been as a family.[12]

The next time you find yourself traveling rocky roads alone, remember Becky's recipe. Tears, laughter, prayer, and friends can sweeten any bitter trail—and with no added calories!

Food for Thought

- Becky's recipe for healing from a tough season in life is prayer, friends, laughter, and tears. What are your thoughts on her recipe? What ingredients would you add, if any?

- Crying is cathartic. It releases sadness, lifts your mood, and gets rid of unhealthy toxins. Are you okay with having a good cry? Does it come easily, or do tears come hard for you? Why?

- Laughter is healing. What is one thing you can do today to bring more humor into your hard times?

- Research says that prayer makes a measurable difference in the health and well-being of people who pray. Do you agree? How has prayer helped you in your life, in your pain, in your hardest times?

- Do you currently have close friends to share prayers, laughter, and tears on life's rocky road? If not, what are some ways to cultivate like-minded friends?

Because *Real Women*
Don't Need a *Cookbook*

Three-Minute Chocolate Cake in a Mug

Sometimes dubbed "the most dangerous cake in the world," this recipe has made its way from e-mail inbox to inbox, satisfying cravings for something chocolate in no time, with ingredients most of us have on hand. I made this today with my grandsons, who thought it was mighty cool! And this nonny was duly impressed as well. Makes enough for two servings, and best served warm with vanilla ice cream!

1 large coffee mug

4 tbs. flour (plain, not self-rising)

4 tbs. sugar

2 tbs. cocoa

$1/8$ tsp. baking powder

$1/8$ tsp. salt

1 egg

3 tbs. milk (may substitute strong coffee, instead, for mocha flavor)

3 tbs. oil

2 tbs. chocolate chips (optional)

1 tbs. chopped pecans

Small splash of vanilla

Add dry ingredients to mug and mix well. Add the egg and mix thoroughly. Pour in the milk and oil and mix well. Add the chocolate chips and/or nuts (if using) and vanilla, and mix again.

Put the mug in the microwave and cook for around two minutes. (Depending on the strength of your microwave, you may want to cook it for a little less or a little longer.) It is best not overcooked. Remove from mug and share half with a friend, husband, child, or grandchild—if you are in a sharing frame of mind. A dollop of vanilla ice cream makes it extra special. A squiggle of chocolate syrup on top of that makes it decadent.

—Becky, Denver, Colorado

Want Sweet Change?
Put It on the List

· · · · · · · ·

Every morning, put *eating chocolate*
at the top of your to-do list. That way,
you'll always get one thing done.

I love lists. I have so many lists that I have lists to manage my lists.

One day shortly after K and I broke up, I made a list of reasons I didn't want to be with him anyway. Some were marginally valid. Others were hugely exaggerated. A good many, truth be told, were completely fictitious, which were, of course, my favorites.

(Don't pretend you've never written this kind of list. I'm guessing you were probably thirteen at the time, but who says a girl has to give up a perfectly good breakup coping skill just because she graduates from junior high?)

But I digress. Back to my story.

The good news is that making my list made me feel better. The bad news is that it made me feel so much better I got a little carried away. My list so inspired me that I wrote K a letter saying I was glad we'd broken up and telling him not to call me in the future. And I meant it too. At least until the postman drove away with the envelope.

But don't let this story sour you on the benefits of lists. Lists are good. It's the envelopes and stamps that can get you into trouble.

How else do I use lists?

In addition to using them to manage my emotions (the occasional overreaction duly noted), I use lists as roadmaps to help me reach my goals. These lists usually contain steps I need to take in order to make some crazy dream or scheme come true. Like, for example, my e-magazine business.

❧ Sweet Secrets ☙

Q: What's your secret to a sweeter journey on the rocky road of life?

A: When I'm going through a tough time and need a little sweetness, I pick up a Christian novel. It helps me from obsessing over what's bothering me. Or I call a friend and talk it out. But most of all, I turn to the Bible, especially the Psalms (like Psalms 19, 23, 37, 42, 63, 103, and 139). I also like 2 Corinthians—chapter 4 in particular—when I'm facing something tough.

—LINDA HARRIS, COLORADO SPRINGS, COLORADO

I came up with this idea about a year ago. The plan was to create an e-mail magazine featuring six professionals as columnists. I would help each of them write an article and create an ad promoting his or her business. I would design the magazine, then help all six professionals send it to their own e-mail list of clients and contacts and...voilà! We'd end up with a readership of hundreds, even thousands, and every professional would get the chance to have his or her article and ad seen by hundreds of potential new customers.

The first thing I did was make a list of all the steps I needed to take this concept from neat idea to solid business. (I had first come up with this idea when I was dating K. In fact, he was supposed to be my first client. When we stopped seeing each other, I came close to walking away from the idea. But when I reread my own list, I was inspired all over again and decided to move ahead.)

I took my idea to insurance agents and bankers and bakers, lawyers and bookstore managers and hairstylists, and even an acupuncturist. While I was trying to find the right mix of businesses to feature, I returned frequently to my list for direction. One of the steps I'd written down was this: *Create an office space with six desks so I have a place to put my staff as my business grows.*

I called my friend John. "Hey, I'm going to look at office space for rent this weekend. Wanna come along?"

"Wow!" John sounded excited. "So you got your first clients?"

"Nope."

"Any money coming in?"

"Not a penny."

"Employees?"

"Not exactly."

"Then why do you need office space?"

"I also need six desks," I said.

"Fine. I'll bite. Why do you need office space and six desks?"

"It's on the list."

John agreed to go with me to look at office space. He managed to act fairly supportive despite the fact that he, oddly, had slapped a strip of duct tape across his mouth. Eventually I came to the conclusion that it was too soon to rent an office, and John ripped off the tape and breathed a sigh of relief. He confessed, "I was trying not to say anything negative, but if you'd decided to sign a lease, I would have had to stage an intervention."

Okay, he didn't *really* seal his mouth with tape. But he did tell me those exact words. And he was right. I didn't have any clients or money or a single employee. It was way too soon to put six desks in rented office space.

I decided to put six desks in my house instead. I borrowed several desks from my dad and bought the rest off Craigslist. I moved my computer downstairs to my new "office" and bought a second computer, used, for a hundred bucks. Then John gave me a computer he wasn't using, bringing the number to three.

By then I had my first client. The rest were soon to follow.

One day Mame walked downstairs and into the new, six-desk office area. She looked at the desks and computers. We were a week away from our first issue going out to nearly two thousand readers. I was at one desk, editing articles. Kacie was at another desk, creating ads. Another young woman, Bekah, was at the third computer, uploading e-mail lists.

Mame shook her head. "Lots of people get ideas," she said. "But when *you* get an idea, you actually do it!"

I grinned. "It's all in the list."

What's the Plan?

Lists aren't just for heartaches or for businesses. I love the following list, e-mailed to me by a woman who escaped an abusive relationship. But before she gave me her list, Alexis told me her story:

> I fled an abusive relationship in 2004 and found that when I reached out to the local domestic-violence shelter, there was no help. They turned me away because of my batterer's occupation. I hid my car at the train station and did what I could to stay below the radar, but since my batterer was a private investigator, it proved difficult to escape. Being physically separated was not freedom, as I became a target of cyberstalking and traditional stalking.

Alexis admits that finding freedom and healing was not easy, but wrote, "Here are some things I did that worked well and that I continue to use to this day to heal."

1. *Clean out the trash.* I removed people from my life who were not supportive—even family members! I did this because I realized that I would be only as strong as my weakest link. I found out quickly that many people in my life were actually adding to the burden I was carrying, so cleaning house in business and my personal life became imperative.

2. *Allow time to heal and to feel the anger, feel the pain, and to not be ashamed of bad days.* Life is not a Hallmark card: not every day is easy for anyone, and not everyone heals in the same way. I found this out the hard way, because I tended to compare myself to others and to feel less than human for

having feelings or troubles. All of that led to self-doubt and low self-worth. Once I began to realize that my emotions were not just okay but real and part of the healing process, I overcame and healed much more quickly.

3. *Enjoy the simple joys of life and give a little to get a lot.* I learned quickly to enjoy simple things that didn't cost me anything. I found these things not only brought me joy, they were also easy to find once I began to notice them: the sun on my face, a star-filled sky at night, a friendly smile from a passerby, or even the lady who held the door for me on the rainy day at the post office.

4. *I also volunteered* with a local crime victims' organization and tried to do more for others. By keeping busy, enjoying the simple joys of life, and helping others, I healed much faster.

Today Alexis Moore is the founder of Crime Victim Organization Network and a director for a national crime victims' organization. She is also an advisory board member of the Beginning Over Foundation and a director for Women's Legal Resource Foundation. Finally, Alexis is president of Survivors in Action (SIA), a nonprofit national advocacy group that supports victims and the families of victims of any crime, including domestic violence, identity theft, elder abuse, cyberstalking, stalking, child abuse, rape, and sexual assault.

On the SIA website, Alexis wrote, "Other national organizations typically help victims at specific points in their victimization cycle—such as when they first report the crime or in writing parole opposition letters—leaving 'gaps' in needed services. SIA is the only organization that fills the gaps, providing support through all stages of the journey from victim to survivor, with no time limitations, cut-off dates, or conditions. Our mission is to ensure that no victim anywhere in the world is left behind."[1]

When you take the right steps, it can change a lot of lives, starting with your own.

Lists to Help You Beat Depression

One evening my friend Nikki and I found ourselves sitting in a coffee shop talking about how we both had survived bouts with clinical depression. I asked, "So what do we do if we feel ourselves getting depressed again? Are there actions we can take that can make us feel better and keep us from that slippery slope again?"

Nikki said, "Gardening. When I'm gardening and the sun's on my shoulders and my hands are in the dirt, I feel better."

I said, "Counseling."

Nikki said, "Taking time for myself."

I reached for a napkin and a pen. "Go on," I said.

We came up with more than a dozen things that helped us feel better, and I stuck the list in my purse. Months later someone came across the list and said, "Is this an outline for your next book or something?"

Suddenly I found myself looking at that list in a whole new light. "It wasn't supposed to be," I said, picking up the list and reading it for the first time in months. "But it could be..."

The list became the outline for my book *Just Hand Over the Chocolate and No One Will Get Hurt*. It has helped more than one hundred thousand women seeking ways to feel better on days they find themselves feeling stressed or blue.

What was on the list? Here's an abridged version:

- Plant a garden.
- Take a minivacation.
- Talk to a friend.

- Whine for fifteen minutes (then stop whining and go do something productive).
- Sing the theme song from *The Brady Bunch*.
- Chase a dream you've always wanted to pursue.
- Find a way to simplify a part of your life.
- Find some time alone.
- Forgive someone (maybe even yourself).
- See a counselor.
- Laugh.
- Practice healthier, happier thoughts.
- Learn to set better boundaries.
- Make peace with your feelings about your body.
- Consider the needs of your soul.

Depression's a tough one. Just yesterday I was on Facebook when one of my readers, a woman named Jessica, IM'ed me and wrote, "Do you normally talk to strange people like me on fb who are suffering from everything? LOL I've been having some issues lately and am reading your book Only Nuns Change Habits Overnight...awesome as usual...but I feel like I really could use some advice."

We chatted about depression, then, because that's what Jessica was struggling with. I suggested three things she could do to begin to get the help she needed. Three things might not seem like a very long list, but when you're just getting started on a journey toward health, wholeness, or healing, sometimes making a list of baby steps is the best way to begin.

I remember another time when I made a list to deal with depression, this time my own. One morning I was putting on my socks and shoes when it dawned on me that one of my socks was too thick for my shoe. This little challenge so overwhelmed me, the next thing I knew, I had collapsed, weeping, onto the couch. As I bawled, it occurred to me that most people aren't defeated by a single sock. In fact, lots of people not only handle this same challenge every morning with finesse, many of them also dress themselves fully and even go on to do productive things with the rest of their day. But this small challenge left me feeling exhausted and overwhelmed. It was an eyeopening moment.

So what do we do when it dawns on us that we're not coping particularly well? They say knowledge is power, and I tend to agree, so the first thing I did when I dried my eyes after my little bawlfest was put aside my denial and admit that I was depressed.

The second thing I did was try to get a handle on what this news flash really meant. After all, if knowledge is power, then perspective is power harnessed. What meaning was I going to assign to my little discovery? I decided that no matter what I was feeling right then (which happened to be hopeless and fatigued) my feelings were *not* an accurate portrait of my life or my future. I embraced the viewpoint that at that very moment the wiring connecting my body to my brain

❧ Sweet Secrets ❧

Q: What's your secret to a sweeter journey on the rocky road of life?

A: Have a good cry. Curl up with my kitties and take a nap. Pray desperate prayers. Listen to some soothing, uplifting music. Go karaoke-ing.

—MAYME SHROYER

was faulty, kinda like a broken thermostat, and that I needed to do whatever it took to get it fixed, so I could start measuring my life in a healthy, accurate fashion once again.

The third thing I did was let someone who loved me know that I was having a hard time. Letting people who care about us know when we are struggling is a great step. I picked up the phone and called one of my sisters, telling her I realized I was depressed and that I was going to do something about it.

Later, I made a list of the three baby steps that had helped me move off my soggy couch and into action. The next time you feel numb or blue—and find your lifestyle hamstringed as a result—try this:

1. *Forget the denial.* If you've been depressed, admit it. If you're not sure, talk to your doctor or visit www.depression-screening.org and take the online evaluation.

2. *Be intentional about what perspective you embrace and what meaning you assign to your depression.* For example, don't tell yourself you're a mess and will never be whole again. Instead, embrace the perspective that your depression is *not* an accurate reading of your future and that your emotional thermostat is wonked but fixable. This viewpoint will not only make you feel better, it's also the truth!

3. *Take one action!* Make an appointment to see a doctor or call someone who cares and tell him or her you're depressed. Talk about further steps you can take to address the problem.

There you go. Yet another list that can help you get on the path toward healing the next time you feel numb and overwhelmed. Depression is treatable. Most people have seasons when they get depressed, but no one has to stay there. If and when you experience depression, there's hope. You *can* climb out of the pit, one baby step at a time. And that's true even if you *are* wearing only one shoe.

Why Do We Love Lists? Let Me Count the Ways...

Why is making a list a great way to sweeten a bitter journey? Here's a list of reasons we love lists:

1. *Lists bring order to chaos.* I've always believed that if we can make sense of our lives on paper, we have a better hope of making sense of our lives in real life.

2. *Lists put us in a calmer state of mind.* The act of sitting down with pen and paper and calming ourselves enough to think and write engages a different part of our brains than we do when we are upset and panicking. The one part of the brain is called the panicking part. The other is called the writing part. See how different they are? Okay, fine. I don't really know anything about which part of the brain we engage when we write. But I do know that, at least for me, it's hard to panic and write at the same time (but maybe that's because running around the house screaming and flailing my arms makes it hard to reach the keyboard).

3. *Lists help us remember things.* You know how some people suggest tying a string around your finger to remember something? That's ludicrous. Strings don't hold a candle to lists. Once I had to remember five things. I tied five strings to my fingers. I couldn't remember which string went to which thing until I made a list of all the strings. See what I mean? When it comes to remembering important things, lists rule.

4. *Lists are like snapshots of our brains* (thank goodness, they're not in color). You know when you get a fruitcake along with a new photo Christmas card from Uncle Zeke and Aunt Zelda and you feel a surge of closeness (from the snapshot, not the fruitcake), even though you haven't seen these relatives since you were ten? Well, I've never seen my brain in real life, so it's hard for me to generate that intimate, close feeling toward this particular organ. But sometimes at night, when I can't sleep because my thoughts are racing, I'll grab paper and pen and write everything down. A long, random list helps corral the rogue worries long enough for me to get some sleep. And before drifting off, I look at the list fondly and think, *This is my brain on paper.* It's the next best thing to a snapshot, and a lot less expensive than an MRI. Maybe next Christmas I'll send it a fruitcake.

5. *Lists can make us laugh…and cry.* I'm thinking here about David Letterman's famous Top Ten lists, which always make me laugh. The list that made me cry, however, was one of my own to-do lists. Once, I came across a nine-month-old list. I cried when I saw it because, when I compared it to my current to-do list, I realized they were virtually identical. Not one thing on my old list had been completed in nearly a year! Staring at the lists, I vowed that I would never let this happen again. (Now I write *Eat chocolate today* at the top of every list. No matter how many things I fail to accomplish, I can always cross at least one item off my list.)

6. *A list can be a road map.* Whether you want to mend a broken heart, start a business, transition out of depression, reclaim your house from clutter, or lose fifty pounds, a list can guide you from where you are today to someplace you'd

like to be tomorrow or soon after. What's the first step you need to take? And the next? And the one after that? Write them down. Returning to your list for inspiration and direction when you feel stuck or off track is a great way to keep from getting sidetracked.

7. *Finally, we love lists because they put resources at our fingertips.* Have you ever made a list of resources you can turn to in a crisis? Me too. Whether a crisis has to do with emotions, relationships, a beauty emergency, or an actual 911 kind of event, sometimes we simply don't have the time or where-withal to go hunting for what we need at the moment we need it. Having ideas or information already pulled together can make all the difference. What kinds of lists of resources are good to keep on hand? At the risk of being *Inception*esque, here's a list within a list:

- emergency numbers
- low-calorie snacks to satisfy your next urge to binge
- a dozen ways to beat the blues
- impromptu fun things to do with your kids
- ten ways to communicate to your husband that you appreciate him
- Bible verses that remind you of the truth about God's providing hand, or who you are in Christ, or the strength you can find in God to make healthy, happy choices

Can a To-Do List Lead to True Love?

Midmorning one Friday I looked at the third item of my daily to-do list and read: *11:30 back dining room at Denny's.* Oops. A friend was starting a lunchtime networking group for entrepreneurs, and the first meeting would begin in less than an hour. I'd have to drive across town, which meant it would be a challenge to get there on time. I debated whether I should even go. In the end I decided I would. It was on my list, after all!

I got there without a moment to spare and found a chair at an empty table. People were milling about, chatting, and finding seats.

"Is this seat taken?"

I looked up. It was K! He pulled out a chair across from me and sat down.

We'd had virtually no contact in eight months. Once, we'd bumped into each other at an art walk. On my birthday he sent flowers. Once, he called and suggested coffee. I told him I couldn't see him because I was getting ready to leave town on business. He said, "When are you leaving?" I said, "Two weeks." He said, "Ah."

I'd appreciated his efforts to stay friends, but they felt like tokens in light of what we'd had and what I still wanted.

And now we were sitting at the same table.

Surprisingly, we chatted casually and less awkwardly than I would have thought. He asked about my kids, about my books, about the e-mail magazine I'd started. He asked how many clients I had. I said, "Five." He said, "You need six, right?" I nodded, deciding not to admit that since we'd planned on launching this project together, I hadn't been able to bring myself to complete the magazine without him.

I e-mailed him later that night. "If you're still interested in being in the magazine, I'd like to have you there."

He called me the next day and said yes.

We needed to make a quick decision about his first article for the magazine. He suggested meeting over coffee. I proposed another phone call instead.

During the next several weeks, I kept our conversations short, handling everything I could by phone or e-mail. He was sweet to pursue a friendship, but I didn't have the heart to chitchat, not when there was still so much left unsaid since our breakup nearly nine months earlier.

One day he said the words I'd been holding out for, the words I'd been waiting to hear.

"I think we need to talk."

We went for a long walk at a park. Sitting on a bench on a hill with a spectacular view of Pikes Peak, he took my hands. "You told me once you felt like there was a glass window between us, and you were always on the sidewalk looking in. I want to break through the glass. I want to see what the future holds for us. Together. No more barriers."

I said, "Why didn't you call me sooner?"

"I guess I wasn't ready. Besides, you told me not to call you. I thought you meant it."

"Of course I meant it. You just weren't supposed to believe me!"

We kissed. We caught up on the nine months we'd been apart. We talked about the future.

That was six months ago. Sometimes he tells me, "I can't imagine my future without you in it. I wonder what the rest of our lives will look like."

I want to say back, "Why wonder? Let's plan. In fact, look! I've already got a list started…"

Food for Thought

ↅ Are you a list maker? What's at the top of your list today? What's not on your list that could give you inspiration or direction to help you get unstuck?

- Lists can help you beat depression. Make a list of things that make you feel better when you find yourself stressed or sliding emotionally downward. Your list might include talking to a friend, journaling, gardening, making an appointment to see a doctor, and so on. What item from your list can you employ today to start feeling better now?

- Knowledge is power; perspective is power harnessed. When you are overwhelmed by your feelings, what is one way to change your perspective?

- When you're having a hard time, are you able to let someone who loves you know it? What would change if you did?

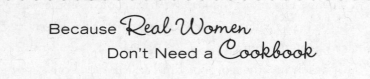

Because *Real Women*
Don't Need a *Cookbook*

Decadent Banana Split

Start with Heavenly Hash ice cream, add bananas chopped up into circles, chocolate syrup drizzled everywhere, chocolate chips, crushed walnuts, and sometimes, for extra sugar I don't need, I top it all off with those colorful minimarshmallows. Yum!

   —Michelle Freeman, New Bothwell,
      Manitoba, Canada

Three Cheers for Chocolate Mousse (or Elk, as the Case May Be)

Sometimes the best thing about getting away is having a chance to see things in a whole new light.

On the same day, Debbie, Lisa, and Suzanne began bombarding me with texts. All the messages said pretty much the same thing: "We're spending this weekend in a cabin at Estes Park and *you have to come!*"

There was no way I could go. It's not that I had other plans; I didn't. I didn't even have to make plans for Kacie; she had already asked if she could spend Saturday night at a friend's house. The problem was that I'd been battling weariness (and even despair) for several months, and I simply didn't have the energy.

My friends left for Estes Park. On Saturday afternoon I asked myself, *So why aren't you with them? Get out of your little comfortable bubble of exhaustion and self-pity and get thee to the mountains!* I tried several times to call my friends to tell them I'd decided to join them, but every call went straight to voice mail. Then I remembered they'd said cell reception would be sketchy. I went ahead and threw a few things in my car and hit the road. I didn't have the address of the cabin where they were staying, so I aimed my car loosely toward Estes Park and kept driving, hoping I'd hear from one of them before I ended up in New Jersey.

Half an hour into my journey, my Check Engine light came on. Worried about breaking down on the side of the highway, I drove back to a Conoco station near my house. I wanted my trusted mechanic, Scott, to take a look.

"You're fine," he said, turning off the worrisome light. "It was nothing. Now get back on the road."

It was the first weekend in October, and as I drove through Denver and headed toward Boulder, the landscape began to change. The closer I got to Estes Park, the more beautiful the world became, filled with fall colors and invigorating mountain air. Sometime in the early evening, the highway took a turn up a hill and as my Explorer topped the hill, I looked ahead at vistas of snowcapped peaks and pine trees and pink sunset clouds. Rolling down my window, I breathed in the chilly fall air and said aloud, "Wow! I'm alive!" My eyes filled with tears. I drove the rest of the way with my windows down and icy air streaming into the car to remind me just how alive I really was.

Eventually one of my friends texted back with an address, and I arrived at the cabin in the late afternoon. Over hot chocolate, my friends entertained me with stories of their first night at the cabin when they were awakened in the predawn hours by the bugling of bull elk just outside the bedroom window. Later, the four of us took a walk before it got too dark and, when we spotted a bull elk and several cows ahead of us, debated whether to keep going or take a detour. While we were still deciding, our bugling friend and his harem meandered off the road and a second bull elk appeared. The two contenders decided to lock antlers, several times, before the interloper veered away, unhurt and unoffended. It was as if the newcomer were saying, *Hey, dude, no harm, no foul. But you can't blame a guy for tryin'.*

Back at the cabin we built a fire, feasted on homemade cheesecake, and played Monopoly. Later, as the flames turned to embers, conversations deepened. I told my friends how depressed I'd been. When they asked why, I struggled to remember all the reasons. I knew it had to do with finances, heartaches, weight, men… And as I shared, I realized the burdens that had been overwhelming just that morning seemed lighter somehow, as if the one hundred fifty miles between home and Estes Park had been too far for my troubles to make the trip.

I went to bed and slept soundly and dreamlessly, not haunted by old hurts or new worries for the first time in a very long time.

Girl Talk and True Confessions

We took another walk in the morning. It was cold enough that the air stung my cheeks and I could see my breath. When I wasn't watching my breath, I was gazing in awe through the pine tops at snowcapped peaks. I was so enamored by my surroundings that I barely glanced down in time to avoid stepping in a steaming pile of elk poop which, oddly enough, looked like Milk Duds.

Back at the cabin we enjoyed a breakfast of fruit, quiche, and leftover cheesecake. Lingering over coffee, we shared more stories. One woman remembered that when she was seven, she had given her mom a pair of dime-store earrings for Mother's Day. Her mother threw the inexpensive earrings away, huffing, "I don't wear trash like that!" My friend said that for years the hurt she felt that day defined her. "If my gift was trash, what did that say about me? That's how I saw myself from that day on, as trash." She said the way she saw herself had determined the men she chose and helped create the problems she experienced in her marriage.

Another woman shared that when she was four, her mother had an affair. "At the time, she was very unhappily married to my dad. They eventually worked it out, but it was a horrible time in their marriage, and I know her affair came out of that pain. The affair didn't last long, but she was terribly distracted and emotionally absent at the time, and I clearly remember how abandoned I felt."

As my friend told this story, I winced, remembering years of unhappiness in my own marriage, and how my pain had at times rendered me distracted and emotionally absent. I thought of my own beautiful daughters and how my wounds had impacted them.

Sweet Secrets

Q: What's your secret to a sweeter journey on the rocky road of life?

A: Eat chocolate, read and sing the Psalms, or dance with my Dad (God). He leads, I keep my eyes shut, and he has never let me run into anything... It's awesome! I dance and sing until joy is released, because it is our strength! I do keep the curtains shut, though.

—JANET

My friend went on to say, "My mom struggled with a lot of things. Her mother was sexually abused, and my mother was molested when she was eight. To this day—and she's seventy, mind you—the first thing she tells people when she meets them is that she was molested when she was a little girl. Last year one of my cousins got married, and as soon as my mom met the new bride, the first thing out of her mouth was her story of being sexually abused. I thought, *How's that for a welcome into a new family!* I've even talked to Mom about this, but she simply can't let go. She has let that single experience define her entire life."

I looked at my friends, women tracing the chain of hurts their mothers and grandmothers experienced and how havoc was wreaked in their own lives as a result. And what about our daughters? Would the chain ever end?

By noon, Debbie, Suzanne, Lisa, and I had packed our things, loaded our cars, and locked the cabin door. The other women had driven up together in Debbie's car, so we hugged our good-byes in the dirt driveway and parted ways.

Driving home, I had a lot to think about. Foremost on my mind was how much better I felt. I felt more alive, as if the weekend had roused my spirit and my brain, waking me up from some sort of stupor. I wondered why.

I remembered reading a column by Dan Miller in which he talked about the brain as an "emergency organ." He said our brains relegate as much as possible to automatic functions, and "it is only when the old order of things won't work any longer that it gets on the job and starts working." He described how easy it is for our brains to switch to autopilot, until jarred awake with an unexpected problem. That's when real thinking begins.[1]

I realized that's what had happened to me. I'd grown weary of trying to solve a series of longstanding problems, and something in me had shut down, gone dormant. My brain? Perhaps. Joy and hope? Definitely.

I thought about the new problems I'd faced this weekend; weird new challenges such as heading out on a road trip with no destination address, figuring out what to do about a Check Engine light, and deciding how close to walk in the direction of mating elk. Facing unfamiliar problems really had shaken my brain (and maybe my spirit) out of its stupor. Suddenly even the old problems waiting for me back home didn't seem as daunting.

The other thing I pondered as I drove south toward home had to do with the chain of pain I spoke of earlier. If I didn't want my daughters sitting in a cabin twenty years from now telling their friends how they'd been impacted by the pain—or even unforgiveness or depression—in their mother's life, what was I going to do about it?

Breaking the Chain of Pain

There's a saying: "Hurt people hurt people." It's true. When people hurt us and we hang on to the hurt, we almost can't help hurting others. It's not our intention, but when we're consumed with nursing our own wounds, it's hard to be sensitive to the needs of those around us.

So why do we hang on to hurt? I think one reason has to do with the economy of loss. Sometimes we hang on to pain in any of its forms, including unforgiveness, depression, or anger, because it's what we received when something priceless—innocence, self-worth, relationship, safety, or even a dream for our future—was taken from us. So how can we give it up? Our own subconscious (and mistaken) reasoning might tell us that, after all, since we paid so dearly for all this pain, it must be worth hanging on to!

Another reason you and I hang on to hurt and anger has to do with identity. If we have let hurt or anger define us for a very long time and then let it go, who in the world are we now?

Finally, I believe you and I can be tempted to hold on to hurt and anger because it's comfortable. It's what we're used to, and while we might not appreciate the pain, at least it keeps us from having to deal with stuff that can feel even scarier, like risk or change or growth.

A New Lease on Life

I don't think there's one path to letting go of pain; the journey can look different for different people. I met a woman, for example, who was beaten senseless and left for dead by a man she had been dating. For months after the attack, she felt powerless and afraid. But over time, she was able to let go of that horrible experience. Her path to letting go included applying to a police academy. Today she's a motorcycle cop with the state of Colorado.

Trust me when I say there's not one thing about this woman—from her uniform and holster to her training and attitude—that says "victim." In fact, she says one of her passions is answering calls for help from women who have been victims of violent crimes or abuse. In addition to doing everything she can do to help them within the authority of her position, she often shares her own story with them. Her message? *Take responsibility for yourself, and do what you need to do to feel safe and in charge of your life again.*

In the pages of this book, we've met other women who have managed to let go of pain by writing or singing, in friendships, prayer, or counseling, and even by adopting a brand-new identity as a beloved child of a heavenly Father. And then there's Laurie. Sharing her story by e-mail, Laurie told me that her path to letting go of pain and low self-esteem included a trip to the delivery room! Here's what she shared with me:

In 2001, my whole world was crashing around me. My best friend committed suicide by blowing her brains out; less than a month later, my husband's best friend finally drank himself to death; my sister was getting married and moving away; and suddenly I discovered, quite by accident, that I was pregnant. Plus, I had a very stressful job: at that time, I was a deputy prosecuting attorney assigned to handling primarily rape and child molestation cases along with the occasional murder and aggravated battery cases.

If I hadn't been pregnant, I'm sure that I would have drunk and smoked and worked myself to death. But while it was one thing to destroy myself, it was quite another thing to harm an innocent child. I began taking better care of my body and entered the healthiest period of my life since I was a child.

I never told anyone, but I desperately wanted my child to be a boy. It didn't matter how far we'd come toward gender equality, the world's yardstick was still male. Females could never quite measure up. How could I wish my own inadequacies upon my child?

In September 2001 I was blessed with a beautiful, healthy daughter. Holding her in my arms, caring for her and loving her with all my heart, had a tremendous healing effect upon me. I had once been a child just like her. Why did I believe there was something innately wrong with me?

Through loving and nurturing my daughter, I finally learned to love and nurture myself. This simple act of loving has transformed my life emotionally and spiritually. I finally understood that the key to the Golden Rule (love your neighbor as yourself) was loving myself. And as I've learned to accept and love myself, I've discovered that the world isn't divided up neatly into "good guys" and "bad guys." We're all neighbors. And thanks to my daughter, I can truly love my neighbor as myself.[2]

I don't know what path you've taken in your journey to let go of pain. Maybe you're still trying to find that path. But if there's one universal truth we can hang on to, I'm convinced it is this: one way you and I can avoid becoming old women who define ourselves by the hurts of a lifetime is to believe there *is* a path to wholeness. All we have to do is find it and then do something. Even if we don't know exactly how to get from where we are to where we want to be, we can take a step in the right direction. Kind of like what I did on that Saturday afternoon in October when I didn't know exactly how to get where I was going. I aimed the car in the right direction and forged ahead anyway.

So please, take a step in the right direction. Call a counselor. Read a book. Talk to a friend. Take a class. Tackle an unfamiliar problem and wake up your brain. Stop thinking of your pain as the thing that defines you or as a thing that's somehow safer than taking a risk and moving toward change and growth. Roll down your windows, even in the autumn chill, and flood your car with the freshest air you can find. Love someone deeply and, in the process, remember that you're worthy of love.

Most important, don't give up. And if, on your journey, you come across a pile of elk droppings, proceed with caution. That stuff ain't chocolate.

Food for Thought

- Is there a heritage of hurt in your life? What steps are you willing to take to break the chain of pain?
- Do you feel like your pain determines your identity? If so, what are you ready to do about it?
- Are you a person who tends to hang on to hurt? What are some reasons people have a hard time letting go of hurt and anger?
- When we're overwhelmed by problems, we tend to shut down or feel emotionally dead. What is one thing you can do to feel more alive—to wake up your brain?

Because *Real Women* Don't Need a *Cookbook*

Note: They say women are from Venus and men from Mars... Well, John Boyd really *is* from Mars. Or at least he had Mars as a client. He wrote:

I'm a big chocolate fan. I'm an attorney and actually used to do patent work for Mars and couldn't believe I got paid to do it. Here are two of my favorite suggestions:

Tip 1: Drip chocolate shell syrup (the kind that hardens when chilled) onto a banana and put it in a freezer for a few minutes to harden.

Tip 2: Dip the tip of a banana into a cocoa mix (like Nesquik), bite, and repeat.

—John Boyd, Ridgefield, Connecticut

P.S. Since mini M&M's are made with very dark chocolate, they have a lot of polyphenols in them (just like red wine does), making them very likely good for you. (Or at least that's what I tell myself.)

Empowering Words That Are Sweeter Than Honey

When you're burned out, worn
out, and in need of serious relief,
there's a remedy that's not only
sweet but calorie free!

What do you do when you're burned out, stressed, or depressed beyond what you think you can handle? Where do you turn for relief?

I always turn to tofu and exercise. Just kidding.

Unfortunately, when I'm tired and stressed, the things I crave tend to be expensive, destructive, or fattening. Like the time I was depressed and threw a party for a hundred people with a live band, a haunted hallway, and an entire room devoted to mirrors and black lights. Or like the night I was packing for a speaking engagement in New York and decided I needed to take a break for a couple of hours. I grabbed the Sawzall and took down a hallway wall. Or like the time I was feeling stressed over a book deadline and went online and found someone selling twenty-nine place settings of a dinnerware pattern I don't own and don't particularly like, but they were such a good deal (only sixty dollars!) that I bought them anyway.

And don't even get me started on coping techniques that involve chocolate!

On second thought, why not? After all, it's hardly a secret that when stressed or upset we can find ourselves craving chocolate and other sweets. And it turns out there's a good reason why we do: When we're stressed, our bodies produce more of the hormones cortisol and adrenaline. These hormones take sugar out of the liver and rush it into the bloodstream in case the body needs a quick burst of energy. The problem is, once this happens, our bodies feel a strong urge to replace the missing sugar. Voilà! Instant craving.

How far are we willing to go to satisfy a sweet tooth?

Tila from Crescent City, Florida, eats chocolate chip cookies…in a sandwich. With mayonnaise.

Tina, out of Louisiana, says she loves M&M's dumped into a bag of cheddar-and-sour-cream-flavored Ruffles.

Finally, Gary, from Illinois, says he's willing to go as far as eating Oreos with salsa.[1]

However we get a sugar fix, craving something sweet when we've been stressed beyond what we think we can handle isn't as random as it may seem. In fact, it's rooted in the way we are made.

Looking for Relief in All the Wrong Places

There were a lot of reasons Jan Dravecky felt as bad as she did. In an interview, she told me: "I felt like a prizefighter who kept getting knocked down. I was thirty-three years old, suffering from memory loss, couldn't eat, couldn't sleep. In fact, I'd completely lost my zest for life. And then I started having five to seven panic attacks a day."

In the twelve years Jan had been married to her high school sweetheart, Dave Dravecky, it seemed they had faced one challenge, loss, or heartache after another. Jan shared with me all she ever wanted was a normal life. She knew her fiancé played baseball and loved the sport, but so did all the players on the college baseball team. It didn't mean any one of them would end up as a professional ballplayer.

So when Dave was drafted by the Pittsburgh Pirates four months before their wedding day, Jan was devastated. Following her new husband from game to game, city to city, and team to team, in the hopes that one day he might find himself pitching in the major leagues, wasn't the nice, normal life she had envisioned.

When Dave was promoted to Triple-A ball, he and Jan moved to Honolulu with the rest of the team. After the first season, the majors still seemed like a far-off dream, and Jan begged him to quit. She pleaded: "We gave it four years. Can't we go home and have a normal life now?" Dave said, "Give me one more year."

The day Jan gave birth to their first baby in Honolulu, Dave was on the road in Arizona. He got to the hospital an hour and a half after Tiffany was born. Jan comforted herself with the thought that even though Dave had missed Tiffany's birth, at least he'd be home for the next three weeks. Then, while Jan and Tiffany were still in the hospital, Dave got the call he'd been dreaming of: he'd been called up to the major leagues!

The good news was that Dave was to pitch for the San Diego Padres. The devastating news—at least to Dave and Jan—was that he was needed in San Diego immediately. The family had one day at home together before Jan was alone…again. She says a deep sadness and loneliness began to settle into her soul, but there was no time to explore her feelings. With the help of her girlfriends, she spent a few frantic days packing up everything in her house for the move to California. Within six days of giving birth, she boarded a plane with Tiffany to follow Dave to their new home.

With Dave constantly on the road, Jan took four-week-old Tiffany to meet her grandparents in Ohio. It would be the last time Jan would see her mother alive. Two weeks later her mom died of a heart attack, and Jan felt more lost and abandoned than ever. Even grieving

Sweet Secrets

Q: What's your secret to a sweeter journey on the rocky road of life?

A: Look for all the things in your current situation and in your actions that are frankly just comical, and then laugh, because c'mon, it's just plain funny! One example: I fell off a ladder in my garage onto the concrete and broke my hip. I was alone, so I called 911 on my cell phone. When the EMTs arrived, I was lying on the floor in really intense pain, and one of them looked down at me and asked, "Do you know you fell on your Weedwacker?" To this day I believe that EMT still isn't sure why I dissolved into laughter—probably chalked it up to shock or head injury. (She's probably right.)

—JOHN KOITER, COLORADO SPRINGS, COLORADO

felt like more than she could bear, so she tried not to talk about her pain and, instead, threw herself even more blindly into the busyness of life.

Over the next several years, Dave's star continued to rise, and Jan found a rhythm to their crazy lifestyle. She gave birth to their son, Jonathan. Dave played in a World Series, was traded to the San Francisco Giants, and his career as an all-star pitcher seemed the stuff of dreams.

Then he discovered a small lump in his pitching arm, and tests proved inconclusive. A year later the lump was diagnosed as cancer, and doctors removed not only the tumor but also half of the deltoid muscle in his left arm. The prognosis was grim: doctors told Dave he would struggle, for the rest of his life, to remove his billfold from his back pocket, much less ever pitch again.

Over the following months, Dave experienced an inexplicable recovery, going on to pitch a comeback game at Candlestick Park, just ten months after the tumor and muscle had been removed. Doctors couldn't explain how, with half his muscle gone, Dave could do what he was doing. The media and the nation fell in love with the Dravecky story. On November 29, 1989, the *New York Times* called Dave's comeback game "one of the most dramatic moments in sports history." Mail began pouring in from fans around the world. It was more than an exciting, heady time; it was a miracle.

A week later, while pitching in another major league game, the bone in Dave's arm snapped in two. It was a huge setback, although doctors thought the arm would heal and Dave would pitch again. Two weeks later Jan got a phone call from a pastor in Ohio telling her that her dad had dropped dead of a heart attack. Two months later, still reeling from the unexpected loss of Jan's dad, the Draveckys were informed that Dave's tumor was back. On November 13, 1989, Dave announced his retirement from baseball.

Jan's life was still anything but normal. Dave's retirement from the game ushered the Draveckys into a brave new world of media attention, speaking engagements, book tours...and cancer treatments. Jan's burnout and depression only deepened.

She experienced her first panic attack during a trip to Washington DC to meet with President George H. W. Bush, just weeks before she and Dave were to appear on *Good Morning America*. Soon Jan was having as many as seven panic attacks a day. Doctors diagnosed her with depression, but well-meaning counselors told her that she didn't need professional help; she just needed to trust God. In the meantime, Dave continued his yearlong battle against cancer, undergoing radiation, surgeries, and chemotherapy. But his doctors said amputation was inevitable.

It had been twelve years of almost unrelenting loss and crisis. The things Jan had embraced to help her cope hadn't helped at all! Hanging on to her dream of what her normal life was supposed to be like had only deepened her disappointment, and her desperate measures to control the direction of her life had failed miserably. Plunging deeper into busyness to avoid the pain of grieving had only shoved the pain deeper and eroded the shorings of Jan's coping skills.

Where to Go from Here

When you're flat on your back, keep looking up. You're looking in the right direction.

I've always been a can-do sort of girl. I like to think that pretty much anything is possible. In fact, one of my least-favorite sayings is,

"You can't get there from here." That sentence doesn't make sense to me. I figure you can get to anywhere from anywhere, even if you have to make a lot of turns and take a lot of side streets to get there.

But sometimes you really do get to the end of…everything. Your rope. Your hope. It has happened to me. It happened to Jan Dravecky. She told me, "Even my give-a-d*mn was busted." That's as good a description as I've heard in a long time.

I got to that same place last year. One night I picked up the phone and called K. This was shortly after we'd broken up (and a good six months before my rejuvenating trip to Estes Park). I was feeling weary beyond words, and I called him, ostensibly on a whim, but really because I was out of rope. At first we kept the conversation light and caught up on each other's lives. But eventually I told him how discouraged and tired I was. I told him that if life were going to feel like a demanding uphill run for the next twenty years, I didn't think I could make it. Worse, I didn't even care anymore.

He just listened. Then he said, "It feels scary sometimes, doesn't it?"

I teared up. "The only things that keep me going are my daughters. If I didn't have them…" My voice trailed into silence.

"But you do have them, Karen. You do have them and you do care." He spoke so calmly that I felt better just listening to his voice. He talked quietly about all the good things and wonderful people in my life.

It was a reprieve, to be sure. But as the feelings of comfort I got from that conversation began to fade, I was well aware that my troubles were anything but gone, and that weariness remained my greatest nemesis. K and I were still broken up (I thought we were over for good, and it would be almost eight more months before I would discover otherwise). Eventually other friends would come into my life—Bradley, John, Mame, and others—and I still had the love and support of my family. But time and time again, as I dangled at the end of a fraying rope, I found myself crying out to God in the pages of my journal and listening over and over to a single song—"Counting on God"—on the CD player. I was struck daily by the realization that when all was said and done, there was only one Person I could turn to for the sweet relief I so desperately craved.

Promises, Promises

Jan Dravecky told me the rest of her story: "When Dave played his comeback game, we were on top of the world. We felt God's presence in our lives and believed we'd seen the worst, and that life would only get better from there. One year later Dave's baseball career was over, he was battling a severe staph infection in addition to cancer, and I was so depressed I could no longer leave home or even drive."

One summer day Dave took Tiffany and Jonathan to the pool. Alone for the afternoon, Jan finally vented all her anger at God. "I shook my fist at God and yelled, 'A year ago I felt your presence! Now, when we need you most, you're not here! Maybe I should turn to the world for comfort!' Yet even as I shouted those words, I knew the world could offer only temporary relief. For eternal relief, I would have to turn to the Word of God. I couldn't deny the Word of God. We had hidden it in our hearts. This would be our rudder."

Jan admits she was so mad at God that she wanted to run, but she couldn't. She was miserable but realized there was no place to go. Like King David, who wrote these words to God, "Where can I flee from your presence?" (Psalm 139:7), Jan knew there was nowhere to turn but up.

"I decided that afternoon to delve even deeper into the Bible and find out exactly what God's promises were to me. I told God, 'I'm going to learn—*really* learn—what your promises are, and then I'm going to hold you to them!'"

As Jan began to study the stories and promises in the Bible, she was amazed. So much of what she had clung to—the hope of a normal life, the belief that she could control her life, and the conviction that good Christians didn't get angry, sad, or depressed—was just a lie! Now Jan read stories of God-loving men and women who struggled just like she did.

King David himself experienced depression—he was so upset that he couldn't sleep or eat, just like Jan. And Elijah, after the greatest spiritual victory of his life, got discouraged to the point of being suicidal. Reading Scripture, Jan learned it was okay for her to be human, ask questions, cry out, be depressed, and get angry. God was big enough to handle not only Jan's suffering but her frustration and anger as well.

Shortly after Jan began seeing the counselors who would help her walk out of her personal wilderness (instead of encouraging her to deny it), she and Dave accepted the fact that they had lost the battle to save his arm. Dave underwent one final surgery for cancer, in which his left arm and shoulder were amputated. Just as Jan was starting to address her depression, Dave plummeted into a deep depression of his own. And yet their days in the wilderness were numbered. A new day was dawning.

As Dave recuperated from surgery and from the loss of an important part of his identity, mail began pouring in. Soon the postal service was delivering three huge bags of letters every day. People from all over the United States, and even the world, were writing to the Draveckys; many wrote to say they were praying for the family; others asked Dave if he'd be willing to make a phone call to encourage a loved one who had cancer. Still others wrote about their own difficult journeys and asked for prayer and a word of hope.

Jan said, "We didn't feel qualified to help anyone, but how could we not answer these cries for help? We eventually hired someone to help us, and the three of us worked for hours every day just answering the many letters."

What quickly evolved was a full-time ministry of hope that Dave and Jan are still involved in today. Jan says that Endurance strives to do three things. "We validate people's experiences. Our story validates the ugly side of suffering, which includes things no one likes to talk about, like anger, questions, doubt, and depression.

"In addition, we encourage people. People don't have a correct biblical view of suffering. People say, 'But we're not supposed to suffer, right?' Then when suffering comes, they're ashamed because they think they've done something horrible to deserve this; they're in denial and don't get the help they need; or they become angry at God and walk away from a relationship with him. And yet, when you look at what the Bible says about suffering, it's pretty clear that suffering is a part of this life. The Bible says things like, 'Although the LORD gives you the bread of adversity' (Isaiah 30:20–21), or, 'In this world you will have trouble' (John 16:33), or, 'After you have suffered a little while' (1 Peter 5:10). So we know there will be suffering, but that God will be with us and we will be refined as a result. We want to share a correct Bible theology on suffering.

"Finally, we want to give people a hope in heaven. I had so many questions about eternity when faced with my own mortality. The truth is that we're all terminal; we will each die one day. And yet the Bible gives us good news about eternity, saying, 'Therefore we do not lose heart' (2 Corinthians 4:16–18). That's the hope side of our ministry."

Jan remembers hearing a sermon by Charles Stanley about the seven stages of spiritual growth. She says she especially remembers stage six, which, according to Stanley, is the most critical. She told me,

"That stage is called spiritual surgery, and it's when God takes the lies we've believed our whole lives, cuts them out, and replaces them with truth. That's what our years of suffering did for us."

She added, "I so wanted to be in control. I wanted to plan everything. And yet from the day I married David, *nothing* went as planned! The good news is that while many are the plans in a man's heart, our steps are directed by God himself. I'm so very glad, now, that my life never did get back to normal or go as I had planned it. After all, if I'd had it my way, imagine what I would have missed!"[2]

Your Words, Lord, Are Sweeter Than Honeycomb

Are you facing stress, burnout, or depression beyond what you think you can bear? If so, there's a good chance you know exactly what it feels like to crave sweet relief. Sure, you can turn to chocolate or to temporary, feel-good fixes the world offers. But for lasting relief—eternal relief—there's something that is sweeter and more satisfying even than honey.

These are the exact words that King David used to describe the effect that the Word of God had on his troubled spirit: "How sweet are your words to my taste, sweeter than honey to my mouth!" (Psalm 119:103). And in Proverbs 4:20–22, King Solomon wrote that wise words are to be hidden deep within our hearts "for they are life to those who find them and health to a man's whole body."

Finally, in Psalm 19:7–10 the psalmist reminds us of the power, wisdom, and help to be found in Scripture. He reminds us that God's words are perfect. They

- revive the soul.
- are trustworthy.
- make the simple wise.

- give joy to the heart.
- are radiant.
- give light to the eyes.
- are pure.
- will endure forever.
- are sure and righteous.
- are more precious than gold and sweeter than honey.

There is no denying that since the beginning, people just like you and me have found sweet relief (and sometimes even miracles!) by looking *up*. So even as you are brought to your knees on the most bitter of paths, look to God's Word and give him a chance to help you.

Food for Thought

ॐ Like Jan Dravecky experienced, are there things you've been doing to try to manage your pain that aren't working? If so, what are some better options?

ॐ Have you doubted God? been angry with him? experienced depression? Are you confident that God wants you to pour your heart out to him, no matter how severe your emotions?

ॐ How much time have you spent this week reading the Bible? Do you think it would be worth spending more time in God's Word to see how your life might be affected?

ॐ Jan Dravecky set out to learn everything she could about the good things God has promised to give those who follow him and then to hold him to his promises! What might happen if you did the same thing?

ᥱ Do you think God's words really are sweeter than honey and are perfect, life giving, and enduring? If you believe this, why? If not, why not?

Because *Real Women* Don't Need a *Cookbook*

Decadent Grilled Chocolate Sandwiches

My name is Allison and I'm a chocoholic. ☺ One great idea I love from King Arthur Flour is grilled chocolate. It's like grilled cheese, only with chocolate (and, if you're lucky, pound cake instead of bread!). However, in a moment of weakness recently, I simply melted chocolate chips in the microwave and slathered them on a slice of challah. It was *delicious* and hardly any trouble at all. A great quick fix for when you're really jonesing.

Here's the recipe for twenty sandwich triangles. It's a runaway hit every time we make them in the King Arthur Flour test kitchen.

10 slices firm-textured white bread (try our
    Buttertop Bread recipe)

Filling
½ c. heavy cream
6 oz. (about 1 c.) semisweet chocolate,
    chopped in small pieces

2–3 tbs. butter

¼ c. sparkling white sugar (optional)

Bring the cream to a simmer and stir in the chocolate; continue to stir until the mixture is shiny and smooth, heating briefly if necessary to melt the chocolate completely. Let cool until thickened.

Butter one side of each piece of bread. Spread about three tablespoons of the chocolate onto the unbuttered side of five of the slices, leaving a bit around the edges uncoated. Top with the remaining bread. Sprinkle the buttered sides of the bread with the sparkling sugar.

Grill the sandwiches over medium heat until they're golden brown on both sides. Be careful— the sugar tends to burn if the heat is too high. Be sure to wipe the pan between sandwiches. Cut the sandwiches into triangles and serve warm to great acclaim.

Note: Any extra filling can be stored—refrigerated and covered—for later use. It is wonderful reheated and served over ice cream. Nutrition per serving (2 triangles, made with white bread, 120 g): 470 cal, 31 g fat, 7 g protein, 51 g total carbohydrate, 26 g sugar, 3 g dietary fiber, 50 mg cholesterol, 270 mg sodium.

—Allison Furbish, King Arthur Flour

Stop! Don't Put the Chocolate Away Quite Yet

Warning: Endless curves ahead
(and breathtaking scenery too)

Last weekend couldn't have felt more chaotic. On Saturday morning I was on the phone with my friend Kris Harty, asking her how she has handled fortysome years of challenges related to having been diagnosed with juvenile rheumatoid arthritis when she was seven.

In the middle of our conversation, I got another call. It was my sister Michelle. I rarely interrupt conversations to take incoming calls, but seeing Michelle's name triggered a vague memory of something... important. What was it? Kris kindly agreed to hold while I took the call.

As soon as I answered, Michelle said, "Did you get my message yesterday about the fridge man?"

"What about the fridge man?"

"He's coming to your house this morning. In fact, he should be there any minute."

No wonder her name had triggered the feeling that I'd forgotten something. I had recently bought a four-year-old refrigerator on Craigslist for one hundred fifty bucks, and a friend was planning to deliver it. The "new" Whirlpool would replace the decade-old GE in my kitchen, which would in turn replace the Paleolithic Fred Flintstone model sitting in my garage. Michelle had arranged for someone to haul the old fridge out of my garage. I'd been so caught up with working on this book that I'd forgotten all about the carefully choreographed fridge dance that was scheduled to take place very soon.

Mame walked into the kitchen where I'd been working. With a puzzled note in her voice, she said, "Some guy at the door says he's here for the fridge?" I hurried to the front door and apologized to the man, confessing that I'd forgotten he was coming and had yet to clear a path in the garage so he could get to the fridge. He agreed to come back later. Rounding the corner into the kitchen, I found Bradley darting toward the laundry room in his bathrobe, apologetically explaining something about his clothes being in the dryer. Mame was standing by the stove, holding a frying pan and an egg. She said, "He's taking the fridge *now*?"

The whole time I'd been pushing the button on my phone that was supposed to take me back to Kris, repeating, "Are you there?" or, "Can you hear me now?" over and over but getting no response.

I called Kris back, and we finished our conversation just as Kaitlyn showed up with her boyfriend, Joel. The kids not only helped me clear a path through the garage to the old fridge, they also helped me empty the food out of both refrigerators and wash down all the shelves. By the time my friend and his brother arrived with the new fridge, there were vegetables, packets of hamburger, jugs of milk, and containers of condiments on every countertop. The men had barely gotten the Whirlpool inside my front door when one of them got an emergency phone call—his mother-in-law had fallen and broken her ankle—so he rushed out the door to the hospital, promising to return the next day to finish moving my new fridge, now parked obtrusively in my center hallway.

Kaitlyn, Joel, Kacie, and I started putting the food back inside all the fridges, including the one in the hallway. Kacie thought having a fridge in the hallway was cooler than anything her friends had. She kept asking if we could "please please please" leave it there. She was relentless.

I said no.

"But none of my friends have an extra fridge in their hallways."

"No."

"Think of how many gallons of milk we'd have room for!"

"No."

"And all the cool magnets we could put on all the doors!"

"What part of 'We're *not* keeping a fridge in the hallway' don't you understand?"

About that time Bradley opened the door from the garage and walked into the basement. Suddenly he yelled, "Why is there water all over the basement floor?"

My crazy day had started with chaos and ended with a flooded basement. I was dog-tired from cleaning fridges and moving condiments. I felt as if I had lived a lifetime in the past twelve hours and was ready to call it a night. And I would have too, if I'd owned a pair of waterproof pajamas.

Instead, it was time to wade into the basement and figure out what to do next.

What's up with all the bumpy roads? What's wrong with a quiet Sunday drive now and then? Or a scenic cruise on a long, smooth stretch of asphalt? Or a gentle downhill coast? Instead, the bumps in the road keep coming. And coming. And coming. Oh, look, a bend in the road! Maybe there will be a smooth stretch around that corner! Oops, spoke too soon. Look. More bumps.

Of course, I'm not the only woman whose life is filled with small bumps (and big ones too). When Kris and I spoke on the phone last weekend, I wanted to know how she managed the ongoing challenges of living with a physical disability. The first thing she said was that she's learned to plow ahead. Then she told me the secret of how she does it. "Living with a disability puts a lot of limitations on you, physically, emotionally, and socially. If I gave into every limitation, I'd get nowhere at all. So I learned early on to keep going. In fact, if you tell me I can't do something, it just makes me more determined to find a way to do it. I'm going to prove you wrong."

Great attitude, but not always our natural bent. I asked Kris how we get to the place where we can do that plowing-ahead thing instead of the soggy weeping thing I'm more prone to embrace. She shared her

Sweet Secrets

Q: What's your secret to a sweeter journey on the rocky road of life?

A: Crisis = high emotions. The best way I know to reset my emotions is with lots of sleep.

—TIFNEY FIELDS

secret. "It's easy to get immobilized by fear or discouragement. I always remind myself that I don't have to take on everything at once. Instead, I concentrate on doing one thing and one thing only: identifying and taking the very next step."[1]

Doing the Very Next Thing

My friend Mary Kelly told me that the worst thing that ever happened to her, by far, was losing her husband to cancer four years ago. "We were married fourteen and a half years when he was diagnosed, and [he was] dead within fifty-five days," she told me. "He'd just bought a car. He certainly didn't think he had a life-threatening disease."

Mary described Joe as a Vietnam veteran, a Force Recon Marine, and tough as nails. "The only reason we knew he was sick was that his back hurt. We didn't know the cancer had penetrated his spine. He had exposed nerves before he realized what was happening."

Mary said that if anyone should have been prepared for managing the emotions and details of that kind of tragedy, it was her. "I was six months away from retiring from the navy. I'd been a human resource director, and I'd worked in two hospitals. I was used to making high-level decisions and managing crises and details. But Joe's cancer and death knocked me flat. It was beyond overwhelming."

So she started making lists of things she knew were going to have to be done. "When you feel yourself losing the ability to focus and to cope," she told me, "sit with a pen and paper and figure out what you need to do next. Make a list. Even when you feel like you can't get out of bed or off the floor, you look at your list and think, *Okay, I can do this.* One day I had to empty the dishwasher. I remember thinking that it felt as impossible as climbing Mount Everest. I asked myself,

What's the next step? Then I thought, *Empty the forks. What if I just emptied the forks?* That I could do."[2]

Identifying the Next Step IS the Next Step

Isak Dinesen wrote, "God made the world round so we would never be able to see too far down the road."[3] But thank goodness we can always see far enough to take one more step. And from that vantage point, we can see far enough to take the next step. And from there, the step after that.

Kris said that traveling bumpy roads is a lot easier when you trust that with every step you take, a way will be made so you can continue moving forward. I like her advice. It's different from what I'm inclined to do, which is obsessively squint and strain to see where the bumps finally end and the smooth highway begins. But if the road winds, or if there are rocks as far as I can see, squinting and straining are a fruitless and discouraging way to travel.

Are you traveling along a rocky road? Even if you're convinced you're too weary to finish the journey, can you identify the next step you need to take? If so, can you take it? Can you muster the faith to believe that after you take that next step, you'll discover the resources you'll need for whatever it is you'll have to do after that?

Noticing Flowers along the Rocky Road

My basement was flooded, so what was the next step? Bradley decided to drive to Wal-Mart and buy a mop. I decided Wal-Mart was too far away and opted to drive to my mom and dad's house to borrow Dad's Shop-Vac. Both were good ideas.

But the winning next step was the one identified by Joel and Kaitlyn. By the time I returned with the Shop-Vac (and Bradley got home with a mop), Joel and Kaitlyn had not only mopped up the water with towels, they'd ripped up the soggy laminate flooring that was disintegrating before our eyes and carted it outside to the trash can.

And what a blessing for me! People who loved me had stepped in to manage the crisis. Kaitlyn and Joel had started working in the basement, and Bradley's trip to Wal-Mart had been a gift at the end of a chaotic day. It was a day I could easily describe as a rocky road—and maybe even openly hostile territory. But there had also been vibrant blooms amid the rocks, splashes of color and beauty that I'm glad I took the time to notice.

Within a few days everything was back in order and every fridge safely in its place. One night I turned off the lights in the kitchen and my whole quirky family stood in front of the new fridge, admiring the glow of the icemaker light in the door. In the illumination of the icemaker bulb, I could see that everyone was smiling. I even heard a few "oohs" and "aahs." It was a beautiful thing.

Finding Beauty Where You Are

It's one thing to see the lighter side of a plumbing disaster or chaotic appliance acquisition. But what about finding a kind of poignant beauty in *really* hostile terrain, like a lifelong disability or losing someone you love? Is it possible to find beauty in the journey through that kind of wilderness?

Mary Kelly believes it is. "Things can only get so bad, then they become funny. It's a way to cope, and it really helps. Especially when you're hurting and people say all the wrong things, it helps if you can laugh. After Joe died, people kept telling me, 'He's in a better place.'

Eventually I'd quip back, 'Oh c'mon, living with me wasn't really that bad.'"

Mary also remembers the kindness of friends. "I remember every single person who called during that time and left me a kind message, even if I didn't return the call because I couldn't muster the energy. And when Joe was dying, and I was at the hospital night and day, my friends brought me Jamba Juice and Starbucks. Every day. My friends were amazing. I survived on that stuff for a month.

"My friends were amazing because they showed up. People say, 'I know someone who just suffered a terrible loss, but I don't want to show up because I don't know what to say.' Just show up. One of my friends came to my house and changed sheets and vacuumed, and it meant the world to me. You don't have to know what to say. It's about showing up."[4]

No Exits Ahead

Sometimes when I'm on a road trip, I see cautionary signs like these: *No Exits for the Next Twenty Miles, No Services for the Next Forty-Seven Miles,* and *No Gas for One Hundred Twenty Miles.* So I stop to fill up the tank, knowing if I don't, I'll wish I had.

It has taken me a lot of living to realize, on the rocky road of life, there aren't any exits. They just forgot to post the cautionary sign.

Oh sure, some roads are less rocky than others, and there are even short spells of smooth stretches. And there *are* services of sorts, at least in the form of friends and loved ones who'll come alongside and help make the journey sweeter than it would have been without them. But basically, there will always be bumps. And rocks. And even the occasional breakdown on the side of the road. Our travels will never be trouble free, but that doesn't mean they're not worth the mileage.

To make the most of any road trip, what do we need to know? How should we pack? What resources should we keep on hand?

Good traveling companions are a must. So is a good compass. How about sunglasses and flashlights, to prepare us for bright days and dark nights since we'll be certain to experience plenty of both? And let's not forget about the chocolate.

Hopefully, in the pages of this book, you've been given plenty of sweet morsels for your journey. And it is proven advice from fellow road warriors, no less! I don't know if that's comforting to you, but it is to me. We're not alone on the journey. The road-tested secrets and transparent confessions of the women who have shared their stories are proof of that!

Which reminds me. We began this book dismayed by unpleasant ingredients in the messy kitchens of our lives. We're ending it on a road, moving forward despite the bumps, acknowledging beauty even in bitter terrain, accompanied by friends and equipped with the good advice of our fellow travelers.

If you ask me, we've been stepping in the right direction.

What Now?

Would you do something for me? Take one more step. Secrets are fun to keep, but they're even more fun to share. Reach out to someone you know who's traveling a rocky road and share with her one of the sweet secrets in this book, or even a secret of your own.

These days Mary is doing just that, teaching seminars that help people organize important documents so they can be better prepared in case of an unexpected crisis, illness, or death. (For more on what Mary Kelly does, go to www.organize-you.com.) And Kris writes a weekly column and authored a book for health-care providers. She speaks frequently to groups on topics like sticking to your dreams and goals, and persevering through the adversities in your life. (For more on what Kris Harty does, see www.strongspiritunlimited.com.)

You have as much to offer as the rest of us. And I'm quite certain that in your daily travels, you come across fellow travelers who long for sweeter journeys of their own. If your own road is still a little rocky, that's all right. It doesn't decrease the value of your insights. In fact, it makes them all the more precious.

Now get going and start sharing. Someone somewhere is waiting to hear *your* secrets for a sweeter journey on this rocky (but wonderful!) road that we call life.

Food for Thought

- When you're traveling a rocky, dimly lit road, do you tend to look so far ahead that you feel overwhelmed? What difference might it make if, instead, you focused on simply identifying the next step and then taking it?
- Kris Harty suggests getting started, then trusting that you'll find the resources you need to keep taking the steps that will eventually get you where you want to be. Whom do you trust? Yourself? God? The process? What has the most meaning for you?
- Do you believe that you have insights and wisdom that can benefit others on their rocky journeys?
- What's your secret for finding the beauty that's present in every landscape of your life, even when that landscape feels harsh and punishing?

Because *Real Women*
Don't Need a *Cookbook*

Chocolate Molten Cake

I am *all* about creating my own version of a chocolate molten cake. It's warm and laden with hot fudge, drizzled caramel frosting, slivered almonds, and a touch of walnuts for the crowning glory. This is my infamous Bundt cake. Then I rip off the lid of a container of Heavenly Hash, Muddy Sneakers, or Rocky Road ice cream, and use all the might I can muster to get a real scoop out of the frozen mess on the first try. Treats in hand, I sink into my leather love seat and admire the fall sky and the warm colors that God blesses us with by his magnificent paintbrush. Relishing the rocky road that I have traversed, I thank him for his goodness—it is heavenly!

—Laurie Copeman, Cicero, New York

Not-So-Secret Chocolate Secrets

"I crave yummy Ghirardelli brownies, right out of the oven when they're hot and gooey!"
　—Denise, Colorado Springs, Colorado

"My problem with chocolate is that my body doesn't like it, so when I'm craving chocolate, I turn to carob-coated almonds. Mmm, just writing about them makes me want to have a few!"
　—Linda Harris, Colorado Springs, Colorado

"I must share my Silk Light Chocolate ice cream and Grape-Nuts treat. It really, really tastes like a Drumstick! It's a nostalgic chocolate treat with a healthy twist!"
　—Beth Lueders, Colorado Springs, Colorado

"My chocolate snacks of choice are a Snickers bar, or Dreyer's Rocky Road ice cream, or chocolate chip cookies."

—Sue, Colorado Springs, Colorado

∽

"Every woman should have frozen chocolate cookie balls! Simply prepare cookies and freeze them. Then all you have to do is turn on the oven, put them on a cookie sheet, and bake! It only takes fifteen minutes to eat a warm, chewy, decadent bite of chocolate fantasy!"

—Amy

∽

"If I need a chocolate fix, fast, which happens often now that my hormones are all the rage, I hope there's a bag of chocolate chips in the pantry. Chocolate syrup on a spoon works too. If not, I drive to the nearest coffee shop and get a large mocha latte. Ah, the sweet taste of chocolate in a cup!"

—Deb Buckingham, Colorado Springs, Colorado

∽

"The cookie jar in our home was never empty; it was always filled to the brim with Toll House cookies. If it got close to empty, my two sons would go by and rattle the top of the cookie jar to let me know we were about to run out.

"One summer day my youngest son, Bradley (age eight), was outside playing cowboys with a couple of his buddies. I was inside baking their favorite Toll House chocolate chip cookies. When I brought out a dish of warm cookies and milk for the boys, the cookies were devoured in two minutes flat! Then they were back at the door for more. The boys were so cute, I relented and gave the cowboys more warm cookies! Again they returned, begging for more, but I told them they'd had enough! I couldn't make the cookies fast enough.

"A few minutes later the miniature cowboys were back at the door again, this time holding pieces of wood for guns. It was a holdup! They told me to hand over more cookies! But the mean cowboy mother told the little varmints, 'No way!' and I held my ground! I could barely keep a straight face! Twenty-five years later we still tell that story and chuckle at the innocent antics of three little chocolate-chip-cookie-thief cowboys!"

—Carol, Syracuse, New York

Notes

Chapter 4

1. For more on this, see Karen Scalf Linamen, *Only Nuns Change Habits Overnight: 52 Amazing Ways to Master the Art of Personal Change* (Colorado Springs: WaterBrook, 2008).

2. You can see pictures of Kacie's "Ocean Room" at http://stephaniejohnsonmurals.blogspot.com/2010/01/ocean-mural.html.

3. Lewis Carroll, Martin Gardner, *The Annotated Alice: The Definitive Edition* (New York: W. W. Norton & Company, Inc., 2000), 199, 18, 199, 16, 22.

4. For more on this, see Donald Wetmore, *The Productivity Handbook: New Ways of Leveraging Your Time, Information, and Communications* (New York: Random House, 2005).

5. Elson Haas, MD, quoted in Robrt L. Pela, "Inner Cleansing: Every Day, Toxins Imperil Your Health and Fitness," *Men's Fitness,* November 2002, http://findarticles.com/p/articles/mi_m1608/is_11_18/ai_93009047.

6. "Stress and the Brain," compiled by Arlene R. Taylor, *Realizations Inc.,* www.arlenetaylor.org/brain-references-menu/1418-stress-and-the-brain-a-l.

7. Dr. Pamela Peeke, "Influence of Hormones on Weight Gain," *Anne Collins Weight Loss Program 2010,* www.annecollins.com/weight_health/hormones-weight-gain.htm.

8. Kevin Mathias, "Stress and Health: Effects of Stress on the Body," *Buzzle*, Intelligent Life on the Web, www.buzzle .com/articles/stress-health-effects-body.html.

Chapter 5

1. It should go without saying that if you haven't known someone for a long time, then protect your emotions and yourself by not having him around when you're working late at night!

2. "Friends Our Lifelines," *Guardian Health Chronicle*, October 15, 2009, www.myhealthguardian.com/good-for-you/ friends-our-lifelines.

3. Tara Parker-Pope, "What are Friends For? A Longer Life," *New York Times*, April 20, 2009, www.nytimes.com/2009/04/21/ health/21well.html.

4. Results of study cited at "Health Benefits of Having Good Friends," April 2, 2009, http://healthy-lifestyle.most-effective-solution.com/2009/04/01/health-benefits-of-having-good-friends.

5. "Health Benefits of Having Good Friends."

6. Kris Harty, personal interview by the author.

Chapter 6

1. Justus von Liebig, quoted in the *Chocolate & Friends* (blog), October 29, 2010, www.palyne.com/talk.

2. James W. Pennebaker and Janel D. Seagal, "Forming a Story: The Health Benefits of Narrative," *Journal of Clinical Psychology* 55, no. 10 (Hoboken, NJ: John Wiley and Sons, 1999), 1243–4, http://citeseerx.ist.psu.edu/viewdoc/summary?doi=10.1.1.58.8591.

3. Pennebaker and Seagal, "Forming a Story: The Health Benefits of Narrative," 1244.

4. Chuck Maher, personal interview by the author, December 6, 2009. For more information on how to protect your investments without supporting companies that maintain values contrary to your own, go to www.chuckmahercfp.com.

5. Chuck Maher, personal interview by the author, December 6, 2009.

6. Matthew Kelly, *The Seven Levels of Intimacy: The Art of Loving and the Joy of Being Loved* (New York: Fireside, 2007), 16.

7. Emily, personal interviews by the author.

8. Kelly, *The Seven Levels of Intimacy,* 9.

9. Emily, personal interviews by the author.

Chapter 7

1. Emily, personal interviews by the author.

2. Harry Thacker Burleigh, "Sometimes I Feel Like a Motherless Child," copyright © 1918 G. Ricordi & Co.

Chapter 8

1. Erik Weihenmayer, telephone interview by the author, August 31, 2010.

2. Cathy Flandermeyer, personal interview by the author, August 29, 2010.

3. Mad Dog, "This Is Your Life, Take Two," *The Mad Dog Weekly,* www.maddogproductions.com/ds_reinvention.htm.

Chapter 9

1. Dave Barry, "Humorous Quotes from Dave Barry's Bad Habits," *WorkingHumor,* www.workinghumor.com/quotes/dave_barry_habits.shtml.

2. Ellen Weihenmayer, e-mail message to the author.

3. *Living Paradox* (blog), http://livingparadox.blogspot.com.

4. Patricia Fragen, e-mail correspondence with the author.

Chapter 10

1. "Pat Boone," *Wikipedia,* http://en.wikipedia.org/wiki/
Pat_Boone.

Chapter 11

1. Henry Maudsley, *The Quote Garden,* www.quotegarden.com/
crying.html.

2. Research from the University of Minnesota, "Tears," *Wikipedia,* http://en.wikipedia.org/wiki/Tears.

3. Mayo Clinic Staff, "Constant Stress Puts Your Health at
Risk," *Mayo Clinic,* www.mayoclinic.com/health/stress/
SR00001.

4. R. Morgan Griffin, "Give Your Body a Boost—with Laughter,"
WebMD, http://women.webmd.com/guide/give-your-body-
boost-with-laughter.

5. For more on this, see William Backus, *The Healing Power of a
Healthy Mind* (Minneapolis: Bethany, 1997).

6. "Prayer: Health Benefits," *Alternative Medicine Therapies,*
http://stason.org/TULARC/health/alternative-medicine/
Prayer-Health-Benefits.html. (Scroll down to see article.)

7. Betsey Newenhuyse and Jane Johnson Struck, personal interview by the author, September 7, 2010.

8. Brandilyn Collins, "My Healing," www.brandilyncollins.com/
healing.html and Brandilyn Collins, personal interview by the
author.

9. Cathy Flandermeyer, personal interview by the author, August
29, 2010.

10. Betsey Newenhuyse and Jane Johnson Struck, "Welcome to Our World," *Betsey:Jane* (blog), July 20, 2010, http://betsey njanes.blogspot.com, and personal interview by the author, September 7, 2010.

11. Ane Mulligan, personal interview by the author.

12. Becky, personal conversations with the author.

Chapter 12

1. Alexis Moore, personal interview by the author. For more information about Alexis Moore's work, go to www.survivors inaction.com and http://groups.yahoo.com/group/Crime VictimOrgNetwork.

Chapter 13

1. Dan Miller, "Wake Up Your Brain," www.crosswalk.com/ careers/11604044.

2. Laurie Gray, e-mail correspondence with author. Laurie is an attorney, child advocate, and author of the young-adult novel *Summer Sanctuary* (Carmel, IN: Luminis, 2010). To read more about Laurie, visit her Web site at www.socraticparenting.com.

Chapter 14

1. Tasty tidbits quoted in Jane Weaver, "Got an Urge for Something Weird and Tasty?" *MSNBC,* www.msnbc.msn.com/ id/23186776.

2. Jan Dravecky, interview with the author. Jan Dravecky has written about her experiences in several books, including *When You Can't Come Back,* coauthored with Dave Dravecky (Grand Rapids, MI: Zondervan, 1992) and *A Joy I'd Never Known* (Zondervan, 1998).

Chapter 15

1. Kris Harty, personal interview by the author.
2. Mary Kelly, personal interview by the author.
3. Karen von Blixen-Finecke was a Danish author who wrote under the pen name Isak Dinesen. This quote is widely attributed to her. *Creative Quotations,* http://creativequotations .com/one/1117.htm.
4. Mary Kelly, personal interview by the author.

Change is never easy— arm yourself with laughter

HAVE YOU EVER MET A WOMAN WHO DIDN'T WANT TO CHANGE SOMETHING IN HER LIFE?

With a good dose of humor and loads of practical advice, Karen Linamen gives you fifty-two ways to turn your dissatisfaction into lasting life change.

GET TO KNOW THE NEW IMPROVED, IMPERFECT YOU!

Stop allowing the number on the scale or the size of your jeans to define who you are. Now you can find the physical and emotional energy to live the life you've always desired—as you reveal a more beautiful, confident you!

Both books include questions for reflection and discussion
Read an excerpt at WaterBrookMultnomah.com